Reader/Writer Notebook

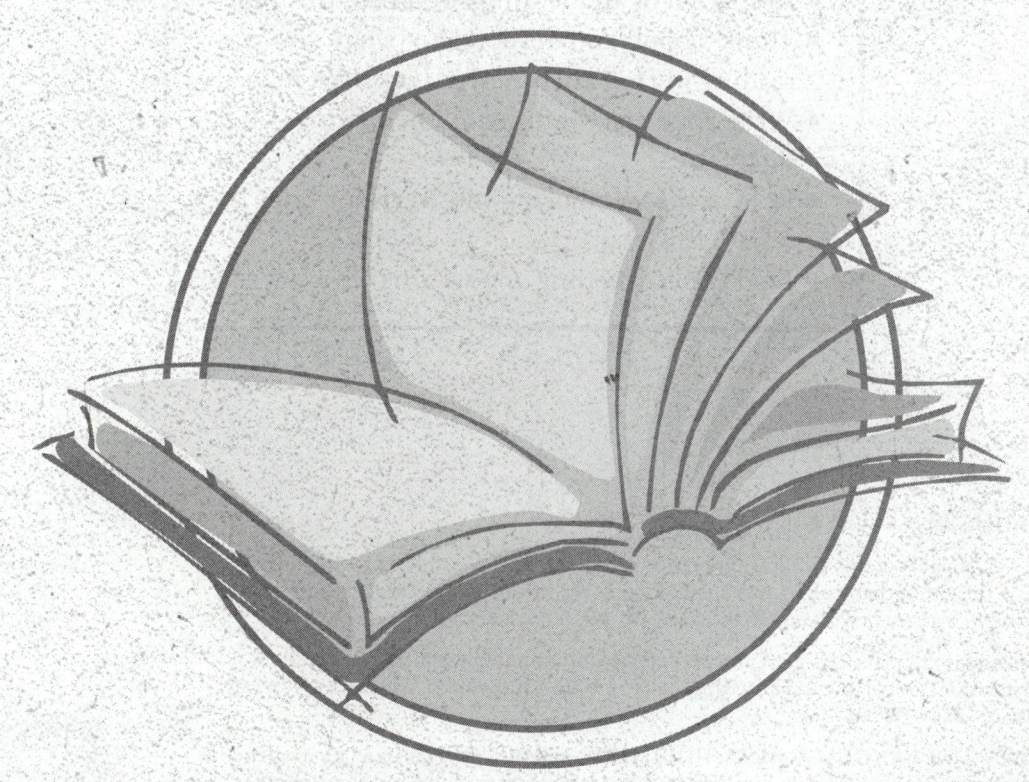

HOLT, RINEHART AND WINSTON

How To Use Your
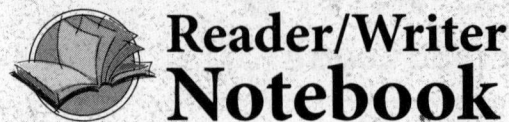
Reader/Writer Notebook

You've been in school long enough to know that you can't write in your textbooks. But, many times, you need to capture your thoughts about what you are reading or write your ideas down on paper. This Reader/Writer Notebook is a place where you do just that.

In this notebook, you'll find space to do the following:

- Take reading and writing interest surveys
- Keep a list of all the things you read this year
- Think about and respond to what you are reading in *Holt Literature & Language Arts*
- Write your first drafts for all the writing you'll do this year
- Record the vocabulary you learn (or hope to learn!) this year
- Find tips for reading and writing

Copyright © by Holt, Rinehart and Winston

All rights reserved. No part of this publication may be reproduced or transmitted in any form or by any means, electronic or mechanical, including photocopy, recording, or any information storage and retrieval system, without permission in writing from the publisher.

Requests for permission to make copies of any part of the work should be mailed to the following address: Permissions Department, Holt, Rinehart and Winston, 10801 N. MoPac Expressway, Building 3, Austin, Texas 78759.

HOLT LITERATURE & LANGUAGE ARTS, HOLT, HRW, and the **"Owl Design"** are trademarks licensed to Holt, Rinehart and Winston, registered in the United States of America and/or other jurisdictions.

Printed in the United States of America

If you have received these materials as examination copies free of charge, Holt, Rinehart and Winston retains title to the materials and they may not be resold. Resale of examination copies is strictly prohibited.

Possession of this publication in print format does not entitle users to convert this publication, or any portion of it, into electronic format.

ISBN 13: 978-0-55-401691-7
ISBN 10: 0-55-401691-5

1 2 3 4 5   179   12 11 10 09 08

CONTENTS

Reading Into Action *by Kylene Beers* 2
Want to improve your reading skills? Here you'll find helpful tips on how to become a better reader.

Myself as a Reader Survey 5
If you want to see how much you improve as a reader throughout the school year, make sure to fill out this survey.

Writing Into Action *by Linda Rief* 6
Want to be a better writer? Here you'll find tips that will help you improve your writing.

Myself as a Writer Survey 8
If you want to see how much you improve as a writer throughout the school year, make sure to fill out this survey.

Reading and Vocabulary

My Reading 10
What do you like to read? Here's a place to record everything you read during the school year so you can track your progress as a reader.

Selection Notes 14
This section provides space to work through the activities in the Preparing to Read and Applying Your Skills pages in your textbook, to summarize the selection, to think about strategies you used while reading, and to jot down ideas for your own writing.

Vocabulary 134
As you read your textbook, keep an eye out for vocabulary words. Make a handy list of words here so you can review them throughout the school year.

Writing

Ideas for Writing 140
Have you ever had a great idea and wanted to write about it? These pages give you space to put your ideas on paper.

My Notes and Drafts 144
You can take notes on whatever you want on these pages, but this section also provides plenty of space to work on your Writing Workshops first drafts and the Your Turn activities in your textbook.

Resources

Word Parts and Academic Vocabulary 188
This handy reference lists all the word parts and academic vocabulary found in your textbook.

Vocabulary Graphic Organizers 192
These eight graphic organizers demonstrate ways to learn the meanings of words and make the words your own.

Reading Matters 200
School is not the only place where you'll need to understand what you read. This resource provides you with strategies for "real world" reading.

Test Smarts 212
Want to be a better test taker? Here you'll learn strategies that will help you ace your next test.

Reading *Into Action*
by Kylene Beers

No matter where you live, no matter what you do, reading matters. Whether you are reading books, textbooks, e-mail messages, Web pages, e-books, comic books, employment forms, magazines, novels, short stories, notes from your friends, or weather warnings scrolling across the bottom of the television screen, reading matters.

These four pages, along with all the information in your textbook, are designed to help you with your reading. Here you'll find specific reading strategies that will help you better comprehend what you read. Use these strategies with the selections in your textbook. Then try the strategies as you read other texts. The more you think about the topics covered in these four pages and practice what's suggested here, the better reader you'll be. That's important because, after all, reading matters.

Starting Out: *Before Reading*

Interestingly, understanding what you are reading begins before you actually begin reading the text! Comprehending what you're reading requires that you connect the topic of the text to what you already know about that subject. So, before you begin reading, you need to begin thinking about the topic so that your brain can begin making connections. Do this by focusing on the following checklist:

BEFORE READING CHECKLIST

Pilots go through a checklist before they begin flying. You too should use a checklist to make sure you are ready to read.

Titles
1. What's the title?
2. What predictions about content can I make from the title?
3. What predictions can I make from the subheadings or chapter titles?

Vocabulary
4. Is there a list of vocabulary words or key terms that I need to look over before I begin to read?
5. Did I divide the vocabulary words into words I know, words I've heard, words I don't know at all?

Special Features
6. What do the maps, charts, illustrations, or timelines tell me?
7. Did I review the information found in the section openers?
8. Can I state my purpose for reading this section? What am I supposed to be learning?

READING INTO ACTION

Moving Through: During Reading

Skilled readers do more than let their eyes move over the words; instead, they are constantly thinking as they read. They are not only keeping up with basic information like what's happening now, but they are asking themselves questions that let them visualize the scene and clarify confusing parts of a text.

Skilled Readers Construct Meaning During Reading By....

Visualizing Can I picture this in my mind? What words help me create that picture?

Questioning What part has confused me? What names or terms do I need to review? Can I put events in the right time order?

Clarifying Should I reread? Read on? Can I point to where I'm confused? Can I explain what is confusing me? Should I look again at graphics? Would looking up a word in a dictionary help? Should I ask for some help?

Seeing Relationships Do I understand the causes or effects of this event?

Inferring What are the big ideas? What conclusions can I make on my own?

Summarizing Can I discuss what I've just read in my own words?

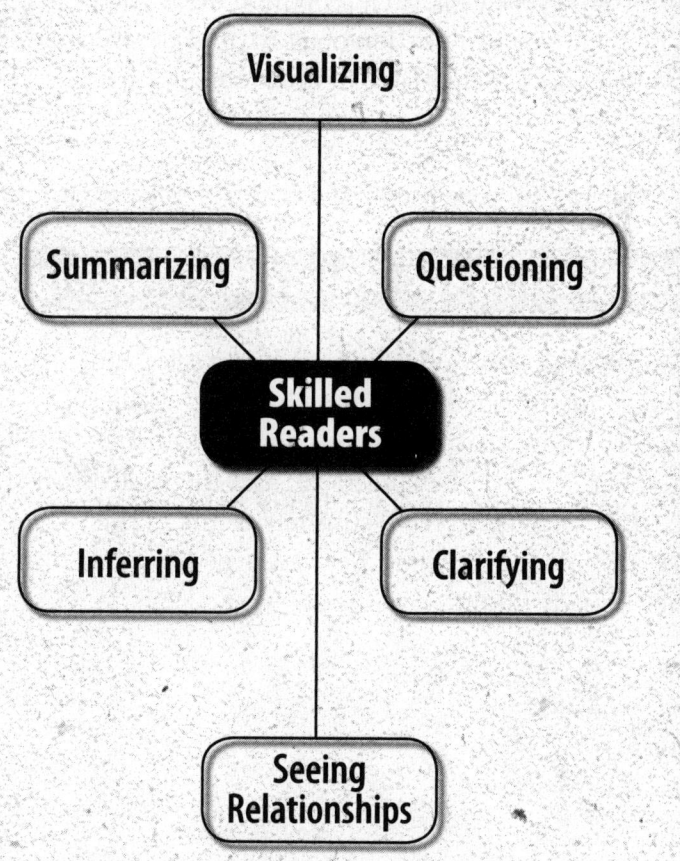

Constructing Meaning When the Text Is Tough

No matter how skilled you are at reading, there will be times when you think what you are reading is too hard. Giving up is one strategy for dealing with this situation, but it's not the best strategy! Instead, when the text is tough, try the following things:

Read a portion of it aloud to yourself. Just like it's hard to figure out what's happening on a television show when the volume is turned down, it's sometimes hard to figure out what's happening in the text when you can't hear. Turn up the volume by reading aloud.

Reread. If your friend says something you just don't believe you respond with a "What!?" and your friend repeats it. That repetition helps you. When you reread a portion of a text, you've given yourself another chance to figure it out.

Read on. Sometimes the best idea is to keep on reading. As you move through the text you'll get additional information that sometimes clarifies what was confusing.

Talk through portions with a friend. Sharing your ideas about what's happening gives you a chance to revise your own understanding.

Look back to the Before You Read page of the selection. There's information there that will certainly help you make sense of the text.

Stop and summarize what's been happening so far. Then read another small section and summarize that. You might be trying to read too much at one time.

See if you can picture the action in your mind And when you can't picture what's happening, spend some time rereading those parts.

Connecting the Dots: After Reading

Even though you've finished reading a selection, you're not finished with the thinking! Skilled readers know that to both understand and remember a text, they need to ask themselves about what they've read, summarize the events, and try to connect what they've learned to what they already know.

Once Finished Reading, Skilled Readers Made Sure They Can…

1. Identify the theme or main idea.
2. Summarize what they've been reading.
3. Identify questions they'd like to ask to know more.
4. Point out parts that are confusing.
5. List important facts, dates, or events.
6. Connect what's happened in the text to another text, to themselves, or to something in the world.

Myself as a Reader Survey

At the beginning of the school year, fill out the first column of this survey. At the end of the year, fill out the second column. Then compare your responses from both columns to see if you are reading any differently or your opinions have changed.

	Beginning of the Year	*End of the Year*
What do you like to read?		
What do you not like to read?		
The best place for me to read is…		
The best time for me to read is…		
The worst conditions for me to read with comprehension are…		
On average, the number of minutes I spend reading per day is…		
If I would characterize my friends as readers, I would say…		
One book I read but think no one should read is…		
I learn about new books from…		
For me, reading is…		

Writing *Into Action*
By Linda Rief

How to be a Skilled Writer

Different types of writing place different demands on you as a writer. Before you begin to write, make sure you understand the purpose for your writing. Are you…

- writing to persuade?
- writing to explain?
- writing to inform?
- writing to reflect?
- writing to entertain?
- writing to pass a test?

Once you are clear about why you are writing, it becomes easier to make sure that every aspect of your writing—your word choice, sentence structure, voice, and structure—serves this purpose. The following tips will help you move through the writing process.

Think before You Write

Have you ever stared at a blank sheet of paper certain that you will never find anything to write? Don't worry. You aren't alone. Often we sit down to write before we know what it is we have to say. Give yourself time to gather ideas—some good, some weak, some promising, some spectacular—before you try to compose your essay. Good strategies for gathering ideas include:

- clustering ideas
- free writing
- talking with a friend
- reading what others have said about the subject
- thinking

Over time you will discover the methods that work best for you, but know that all writers invest time thinking through their subject before they put pen to paper or fingers to keyboard.

Consider Your Audience

Considering your audience means thinking about your word choice. For instance, think about how you talk with your best friend on the phone. You use expressions no one else might understand and probably complete one another's sentences. Now compare that conversation with how you talk to your school principal. The same kind of "shifting of language gears" needs to happen when you write for different audiences. For example, if you want to write a persuasive essay about research that suggests that teens would do better in school if the school day started later, then think about how that essay would shift in language (and therefore tone) as the audience shifts among…

- a younger brother
- the editor of a newspaper
- your teacher
- a school board member
- a close friend

To write effectively, you need to keep your audience in mind.

Get Organized

Every piece of writing has a structure. Can you think of a story or article that doesn't have a beginning, middle, and end? Organization is important because it helps readers understand

WRITING INTO ACTION

what you are trying to say. When your ideas are logically presented, they are more persuasive. When information is ordered clearly, your explanation is easier to follow. Organization can take many forms. You might choose to employ any one of these structures:

- comparison and contrast
- analysis with supporting evidence
- cause and effect
- summary with commentary

The organizational structure of your essay should always reflect your purpose for writing.

Revise!

A few lucky writers seem to be able revise in their heads, but most of us need to write at least one draft and work on that draft alone and with a critical friend in order to produce a piece of writing that others would want to read. Here are questions you might want to ask yourself or a friend to help improve your draft:

- Does my opening engage the reader?
- Does the essay "sound" right for my audience?
- Where might I need to add more evidence, more description, more analysis?
- Are there places where I seem to ramble or get off-topic?
- Does this paper achieve my purpose (to persuade, explain, entertain, etc.)?

Proofread for Conventions of Language

Proofreading, or editing, should happen after you are satisfied you have said what you want to say in the strongest way. Editing is giving directions to a reader as to how you want your writing read. Periods say, "Stop here." Indenting says, "Take a breath, I am moving my ideas in a slightly different direction." Quotation marks usually indicate words spoken.

Reflect on Your Process as a Writer and on Your Writing

In order to begin to internalize and become independent as a writer, think out your process in your finished pieces of writing. Answer for yourself the following questions:

- How did I come up with the idea?
- What and who helped me the most to make it as strong as it could be?
- What problems did I encounter as I wrote?
- How did I solve the problems?
- What did I learn from writers in this book about writing that I tried in my own writing? How well did I succeed at using those ideas?
- What makes this an effective piece of writing?
- What could I do next time to make this kind of writing even stronger?

Remember, writing is hard work. But it's worth the effort. Your words—your thoughts, your opinions, your beliefs—might actually nudge someone else's thinking and change the world a bit.

Gather Your Thoughts

Use this notebook as a gathering place for your thoughts. Not everything you jot down here will become a final, polished piece of writing. But good writing begins with good thinking. This Readers/Writer notebook gives you a space to jot down ideas that you might later decide to turn into longer pieces of writing.

Myself as a Writer Survey

At the beginning of the school year, fill out the first column of this survey. At the end of the year, fill out the second column. Then compare your responses from both columns to see how you have improved as a writer.

	Beginning of the Year	End of the Year
What do you have to do to be a good writer?		
What are all the different kinds of writing you do?		
What is the easiest part of writing for you?		
What is the hardest part of writing for you?		
How do you come up with your ideas for writing?		
What do you think makes a piece of writing good or effective?		
What is the best piece of writing you've ever done? What made it so good?		
What do you like about writing?		
How does reading help you with your writing?		
How does writing help you with your reading?		
What are your goals as a writer?		
What expectations do you have for yourself as a writer?		

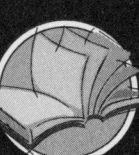

Reading and Vocabulary

My Reading

Just as musicians can quickly tell you music they enjoy playing and athletes can recount for you games they've competed in, readers know what books or stories or articles or Web pages they've read. To help you get in the habit of remembering what you've read, use this chart to keep a running record of everything you've read—from novels to chapters in textbooks to magazines to Web pages.

Note that you should date when you begin and end the reading. Also, jot some quick notes to remind you of your initial response to the reading. They might be as general as "loved this author" or as specific as notes on each chapter. Finally, the last column is a place to make connections. So, if what you read reminds you of another story or something that's happened in the world or to yourself, you could mention it there.

What I'm Reading	Date Begun	Date Finished	Responses	Reading this reminds me of…

My Reading

What I'm Reading	Date Begun	Date Finished	Responses	Reading this reminds me of...

My Reading

What I'm Reading	Date Begun	Date Finished	Responses	Reading this reminds me of…

What I'm Reading	Date Begun	Date Finished	Responses	Reading this reminds me of...

SELECTION NOTES

Title: _____

Author: _____

Page numbers: _____

What Do You Think?

QuickWrite/QuickTalk

Into Action

Think as a Reader/Writer

Find It in Your Reading

Vocabulary

Summary of the Selection

Fix-up Strategies

Explain what you did when it was difficult to understand the text. Did you: Reread? Ask questions?

Keep on reading? Focus on confusing words? Make connections? Jot some notes? Picture it in your mind?

What ideas for my own writing did I get from reading this?

Think as a Reader/Writer

Use It in Your Writing

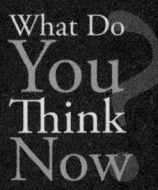

What Do You Think Now

SELECTION NOTES

Title: _____

Author: _____

Page numbers: _____

_____
_____
_____
_____
_____
_____
_____
_____
_____
_____
_____
_____
_____
_____
_____
_____
_____

What Do You Think?

QuickWrite/QuickTalk

Into Action

Think as a Reader/Writer

Find It in Your Reading

Vocabulary

Summary of the Selection

Fix-up Strategies

Explain what you did when it was difficult to understand the text. Did you: Reread? Ask questions?

Keep on reading? Focus on confusing words? Make connections? Jot some notes? Picture it in your mind?

What ideas for my own writing did I get from reading this?

Think as a Reader/Writer

Use It in Your Writing

Selection Notes

Title: _____

Author: _____

Page numbers: _____

What Do You Think?

QuickWrite/QuickTalk

Into Action

Think as a Reader/Writer

Find It in Your Reading

Vocabulary

SELECTION NOTES

Summary of the Selection

$7\frac{6}{9}$

$\frac{3}{10} + \frac{1}{10} \frac{3+1}{10} \frac{4}{10} \times \frac{2}{5}$

$\frac{N}{D}$

Fix-up Strategies

Explain what you did when it was difficult to understand the text. Did you: Reread? Ask questions?

Keep on reading? Focus on confusing words? Make connections? Jot some notes? Picture it in your mind?

What ideas for my own writing did I get from reading this?

① $\frac{5}{7} - \frac{3}{7} = \frac{2}{7}$ ② $\frac{3}{8} + \frac{5}{8} = \frac{8}{8} = 1$ ③ $\frac{5}{12} + \frac{6}{12} = \frac{13}{12} = 1\frac{1}{12}$

④ $\frac{1}{3}$

Think as a Reader/Writer

Use It in Your Writing

SELECTION NOTES

Title: _____

Author: _____

Page numbers: _____

_____

_____

_____

_____

_____

_____

_____

_____

_____

_____

_____

_____

_____

_____

_____

What Do You Think?

QuickWrite/QuickTalk

Into Action

Think as a Reader/Writer

Find It in Your Reading

Vocabulary

Selection Notes

Summary of the Selection

_____
_____
_____
_____
_____
_____
_____
_____
_____
_____
_____
_____
_____

Fix-up Strategies

Explain what you did when it was difficult to understand the text. Did you: Reread? Ask questions? Keep on reading? Focus on confusing words? Make connections? Jot some notes? Picture it in your mind?

_____
_____
_____
_____
_____
_____

What ideas for my own writing did I get from reading this?

_____
_____
_____
_____
_____

SELECTION NOTES

Think as a Reader/Writer
Use It in Your Writing

What Do You Think Now?

SELECTION NOTES

Title: _____

Author: _____

Page numbers: _____

What Do You Think?

_____
_____
_____
_____
_____

QuickWrite/ QuickTalk

_____
_____
_____
_____
_____
_____
_____
_____

Into Action

Think as a Reader/Writer

Find It in Your Reading

Vocabulary

Summary of the Selection

Fix-up Strategies

Explain what you did when it was difficult to understand the text. Did you: Reread? Ask questions?

Keep on reading? Focus on confusing words? Make connections? Jot some notes? Picture it in your mind?

What ideas for my own writing did I get from reading this?

Think as a Reader/Writer

Use It in Your Writing

SELECTION NOTES

Title: _____

Author: _____

Page numbers: _____

What Do You Think?

QuickWrite/QuickTalk

Into Action

Think as a Reader/Writer

Find It in Your Reading

Vocabulary

Summary of the Selection

Fix-up Strategies

Explain what you did when it was difficult to understand the text. Did you: Reread? Ask questions?
Keep on reading? Focus on confusing words? Make connections? Jot some notes? Picture it in your mind?

What ideas for my own writing did I get from reading this?

Think as a Reader/Writer

Use It in Your Writing

SELECTION NOTES

Title: _____
Author: _____
Page numbers: _____

What Do You Think?

_____
_____
_____
_____
_____
_____

QuickWrite/ QuickTalk

_____
_____
_____
_____
_____
_____
_____
_____
_____

Into Action

Think as a Reader/Writer

Find It in Your Reading

Vocabulary

Summary of the Selection

Fix-up Strategies

Explain what you did when it was difficult to understand the text. Did you: Reread? Ask questions?

Keep on reading? Focus on confusing words? Make connections? Jot some notes? Picture it in your mind?

What ideas for my own writing did I get from reading this?

SELECTION NOTES

Think as a Reader/Writer

Use It in Your Writing

What Do You Think Now?

SELECTION NOTES

Title: _____

Author: _____

Page numbers: _____

What Do You Think?

QuickWrite/QuickTalk

Into Action

Think as a Reader/Writer

Find It in Your Reading

Vocabulary

Summary of the Selection

Fix-up Strategies

Explain what you did when it was difficult to understand the text. Did you: Reread? Ask questions?

Keep on reading? Focus on confusing words? Make connections? Jot some notes? Picture it in your mind?

What ideas for my own writing did I get from reading this?

Think as a Reader/Writer

Use It in Your Writing

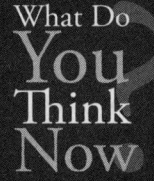

Selection Notes

Title:

Author:

Page numbers:

What Do You Think?

QuickWrite/QuickTalk

Into Action

Think as a Reader/Writer

Find It in Your Reading

Vocabulary

Summary of the Selection

Fix-up Strategies

Explain what you did when it was difficult to understand the text. Did you: Reread? Ask questions?

Keep on reading? Focus on confusing words? Make connections? Jot some notes? Picture it in your mind?

What ideas for my own writing did I get from reading this?

Think as a Reader/Writer

Use It in Your Writing

SELECTION NOTES

What Do You Think?

QuickWrite/QuickTalk

Into Action

Title: _____
Author: _____
Page numbers: _____

Think as a Reader/Writer

Find It in Your Reading

Vocabulary

Summary of the Selection

Fix-up Strategies

Explain what you did when it was difficult to understand the text. Did you: Reread? Ask questions?

Keep on reading? Focus on confusing words? Make connections? Jot some notes? Picture it in your mind?

What ideas for my own writing did I get from reading this?

Think as a Reader/Writer

Use It in Your Writing

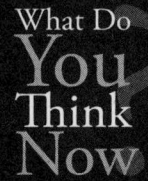

SELECTION NOTES

Title:

Author:

Page numbers:

What Do You Think?

QuickWrite/QuickTalk

Into Action

Think as a Reader/Writer

Find It in Your Reading

Vocabulary

Summary of the Selection

Fix-up Strategies

Explain what you did when it was difficult to understand the text. Did you: Reread? Ask questions?

Keep on reading? Focus on confusing words? Make connections? Jot some notes? Picture it in your mind?

What ideas for my own writing did I get from reading this?

Think as a Reader/Writer

Use It in Your Writing

SELECTION NOTES

Title: _____
Author: _____
Page numbers: _____

What Do You Think?

QuickWrite/QuickTalk

Into Action

Think as a Reader/Writer

Find It in Your Reading

Vocabulary

Summary of the Selection

Fix-up Strategies

Explain what you did when it was difficult to understand the text. Did you: Reread? Ask questions?

Keep on reading? Focus on confusing words? Make connections? Jot some notes? Picture it in your mind?

What ideas for my own writing did I get from reading this?

Think as a Reader/Writer

Use It in Your Writing

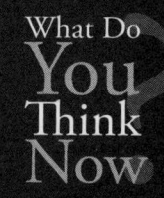

SELECTION NOTES

Title: _____
Author: _____
Page numbers: _____

What Do You Think?

QuickWrite/ QuickTalk

Into Action

Think as a Reader/Writer

Find It in Your Reading

Vocabulary

Summary of the Selection

Fix-up Strategies

Explain what you did when it was difficult to understand the text. Did you: Reread? Ask questions?

Keep on reading? Focus on confusing words? Make connections? Jot some notes? Picture it in your mind?

What ideas for my own writing did I get from reading this?

Think as a Reader/Writer

Use It in Your Writing

What Do You Think Now?

SELECTION NOTES

What Do You Think?

QuickWrite/QuickTalk

Into Action

Title: _____
Author: _____
Page numbers: _____

Think as a Reader/Writer

Find It in Your Reading

Vocabulary

Summary of the Selection

Fix-up Strategies

Explain what you did when it was difficult to understand the text. Did you: Reread? Ask questions?

Keep on reading? Focus on confusing words? Make connections? Jot some notes? Picture it in your mind?

What ideas for my own writing did I get from reading this?

Think as a Reader/Writer

Use It in Your Writing

SELECTION NOTES

Title:

Author:

Page numbers:

What Do You Think?

QuickWrite/QuickTalk

Into Action

Think as a Reader/Writer

Find It in Your Reading

Vocabulary

Summary of the Selection

Fix-up Strategies

Explain what you did when it was difficult to understand the text. Did you: Reread? Ask questions? Keep on reading? Focus on confusing words? Make connections? Jot some notes? Picture it in your mind?

What ideas for my own writing did I get from reading this?

Think as a Reader/Writer

Use It in Your Writing

What Do You Think Now?

SELECTION NOTES

Title: _____

Author: _____

Page numbers: _____

What Do You Think?

QuickWrite/QuickTalk

Into Action

Think as a Reader/Writer

Find It in Your Reading

Vocabulary

Summary of the Selection

Fix-up Strategies

Explain what you did when it was difficult to understand the text. Did you: Reread? Ask questions?

Keep on reading? Focus on confusing words? Make connections? Jot some notes? Picture it in your mind?

What ideas for my own writing did I get from reading this?

SELECTION NOTES

Think as a Reader/Writer

Use It in Your Writing

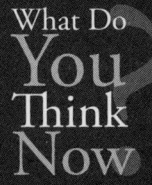

What Do You Think Now?

Selection Notes

Title: _____

Author: _____

Page numbers: _____

What Do You Think?

QuickWrite/QuickTalk

Into Action

Think as a Reader/Writer

Find It in Your Reading

Vocabulary

SELECTION NOTES

Summary of the Selection

Fix-up Strategies

Explain what you did when it was difficult to understand the text. Did you: Reread? Ask questions?

Keep on reading? Focus on confusing words? Make connections? Jot some notes? Picture it in your mind?

What ideas for my own writing did I get from reading this?

Think as a Reader/Writer

Use It in Your Writing

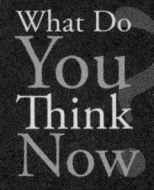

SELECTION NOTES

Title: _____

Author: _____

Page numbers: _____

What Do You Think?

QuickWrite/QuickTalk

Into Action

Think as a Reader/Writer

Find It in Your Reading

Vocabulary

Selection Notes

Summary of the Selection

Fix-up Strategies

Explain what you did when it was difficult to understand the text. Did you: Reread? Ask questions?

Keep on reading? Focus on confusing words? Make connections? Jot some notes? Picture it in your mind?

What ideas for my own writing did I get from reading this?

SELECTION NOTES

Think as a Reader/Writer

Use It in Your Writing

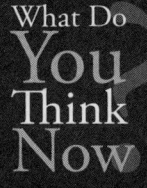

What Do You Think Now?

SELECTION NOTES

Title: _____

Author: _____

Page numbers: _____

Think as a Reader/Writer

Find It in Your Reading

Vocabulary

Summary of the Selection

Fix-up Strategies

Explain what you did when it was difficult to understand the text. Did you: Reread? Ask questions?

Keep on reading? Focus on confusing words? Make connections? Jot some notes? Picture it in your mind?

What ideas for my own writing did I get from reading this?

Think as a Reader/Writer

Use It in Your Writing

SELECTION NOTES

Title: _____
Author: _____
Page numbers: _____

What Do You Think?

_____
_____
_____
_____
_____
_____

QuickWrite/QuickTalk

_____
_____
_____
_____
_____
_____
_____
_____
_____
_____
_____

Into Action

Think as a Reader/Writer

Find It in Your Reading

Vocabulary

Summary of the Selection

Fix-up Strategies

Explain what you did when it was difficult to understand the text. Did you: Reread? Ask questions?

Keep on reading? Focus on confusing words? Make connections? Jot some notes? Picture it in your mind?

What ideas for my own writing did I get from reading this?

Think as a Reader/Writer

Use It in Your Writing

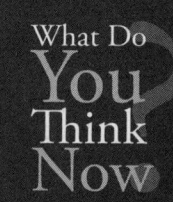

SELECTION NOTES

Title:

Author:

Page numbers:

What Do You Think?

QuickWrite/QuickTalk

Into Action

Think as a Reader/Writer

Find It in Your Reading

Vocabulary

Summary of the Selection

_____
_____
_____
_____
_____
_____
_____
_____
_____
_____
_____
_____

Fix-up Strategies

Explain what you did when it was difficult to understand the text. Did you: Reread? Ask questions? Keep on reading? Focus on confusing words? Make connections? Jot some notes? Picture it in your mind?

_____
_____
_____
_____
_____
_____
_____

What ideas for my own writing did I get from reading this?

_____
_____
_____
_____
_____
_____

Think as a Reader/Writer

Use It in Your Writing

SELECTION NOTES

What Do You Think?

QuickWrite/QuickTalk

Into Action

Title: _____
Author: _____
Page numbers: _____

Think as a Reader/Writer

Find It in Your Reading

Vocabulary

Summary of the Selection

Fix-up Strategies

Explain what you did when it was difficult to understand the text. Did you: Reread? Ask questions?

Keep on reading? Focus on confusing words? Make connections? Jot some notes? Picture it in your mind?

What ideas for my own writing did I get from reading this?

Think as a Reader/Writer

Use It in Your Writing

SELECTION NOTES

Title:

Author:

Page numbers:

What Do You Think?

QuickWrite/QuickTalk

Into Action

Think as a Reader/Writer

Find It in Your Reading

Vocabulary

Summary of the Selection

Fix-up Strategies

Explain what you did when it was difficult to understand the text. Did you: Reread? Ask questions? Keep on reading? Focus on confusing words? Make connections? Jot some notes? Picture it in your mind?

What ideas for my own writing did I get from reading this?

Think as a Reader/Writer

Use It in Your Writing

SELECTION NOTES

Title: _____

Author: _____

Page numbers: _____

What Do You Think?

QuickWrite/QuickTalk

Into Action

Think as a Reader/Writer

Find It in Your Reading

Vocabulary

Summary of the Selection

Fix-up Strategies

Explain what you did when it was difficult to understand the text. Did you: Reread? Ask questions?

Keep on reading? Focus on confusing words? Make connections? Jot some notes? Picture it in your mind?

What ideas for my own writing did I get from reading this?

Think as a Reader/Writer
Use It in Your Writing

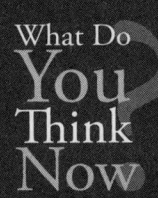

SELECTION NOTES

Title: _____

Author: _____

Page numbers: _____

_____

_____

_____

_____

_____

_____

_____

_____

_____

_____

_____

_____

_____

_____

_____

_____

_____

What Do You Think?

QuickWrite/QuickTalk

Into Action

Think as a Reader/Writer

Find It in Your Reading

Vocabulary

Summary of the Selection

Fix-up Strategies

Explain what you did when it was difficult to understand the text. Did you: Reread? Ask questions?

Keep on reading? Focus on confusing words? Make connections? Jot some notes? Picture it in your mind?

What ideas for my own writing did I get from reading this?

Think as a Reader/Writer

Use It in Your Writing

What Do You Think Now

SELECTION NOTES

Title: _____
Author: _____
Page numbers: _____

What Do You Think?

_____
_____
_____
_____
_____

QuickWrite/QuickTalk

_____
_____
_____
_____
_____
_____
_____
_____

Into Action

Think as a Reader/Writer

Find It in Your Reading

Vocabulary

Summary of the Selection

_____
_____
_____
_____
_____
_____
_____
_____
_____
_____
_____
_____
_____

Fix-up Strategies

Explain what you did when it was difficult to understand the text. Did you: Reread? Ask questions? Keep on reading? Focus on confusing words? Make connections? Jot some notes? Picture it in your mind?

_____
_____
_____
_____
_____
_____
_____

What ideas for my own writing did I get from reading this?

_____
_____
_____
_____
_____

Think as a Reader/Writer

Use It in Your Writing

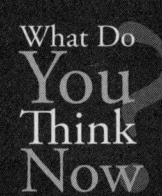

SELECTION NOTES

Title:

Author:

Page numbers:

What Do You Think?

QuickWrite/QuickTalk

Into Action

Think as a Reader/Writer

Find It in Your Reading

Vocabulary

Summary of the Selection

Fix-up Strategies

Explain what you did when it was difficult to understand the text. Did you: Reread? Ask questions?

Keep on reading? Focus on confusing words? Make connections? Jot some notes? Picture it in your mind?

What ideas for my own writing did I get from reading this?

Think as a Reader/Writer

Use It in Your Writing

What Do You Think Now

SELECTION NOTES

Title: _____

Author: _____

Page numbers: _____

_____

_____

_____

_____

_____

_____

_____

_____

_____

_____

_____

_____

_____

_____

_____

What Do You Think?

QuickWrite/QuickTalk

Into Action

Think as a Reader/Writer

Find It in Your Reading

Vocabulary

Summary of the Selection

Fix-up Strategies

Explain what you did when it was difficult to understand the text. Did you: Reread? Ask questions?

Keep on reading? Focus on confusing words? Make connections? Jot some notes? Picture it in your mind?

What ideas for my own writing did I get from reading this?

Think as a Reader/Writer

Use It in Your Writing

SELECTION NOTES

Title: _____
Author: _____
Page numbers: _____

What Do You Think?

QuickWrite/QuickTalk

Into Action

Think as a Reader/Writer

Find It in Your Reading

Vocabulary

Summary of the Selection

Fix-up Strategies

Explain what you did when it was difficult to understand the text. Did you: Reread? Ask questions?

Keep on reading? Focus on confusing words? Make connections? Jot some notes? Picture it in your mind?

What ideas for my own writing did I get from reading this?

Think as a Reader/Writer

Use It in Your Writing

What Do You Think Now

SELECTION NOTES

Title:

Author:

Page numbers:

What Do You Think?

QuickWrite/QuickTalk

Into Action

Think as a Reader/Writer

Find It in Your Reading

Vocabulary

Summary of the Selection

Fix-up Strategies

Explain what you did when it was difficult to understand the text. Did you: Reread? Ask questions?

Keep on reading? Focus on confusing words? Make connections? Jot some notes? Picture it in your mind?

What ideas for my own writing did I get from reading this?

Think as a Reader/Writer

Use It in Your Writing

Vocabulary

While you read, keep track of all the words and definitions you want to remember on these pages.

Vocabulary Word	Definition	page

Vocabulary Word	Definition	page

VOCABULARY

Vocabulary Word	Definition	page

Vocabulary Word	Definition	page

Vocabulary

Vocabulary Word	Definition	page

Writing

Ideas for Writing

These pages give you space to brainstorm writing ideas and what you might want to write. In the first column record your ideas. In the second column record what you want to write.

Ideas	What I want to write

Ideas for Writing

Ideas	What I want to write

Ideas for Writing

Ideas	What I want to write

142

Ideas for Writing

Ideas	What I want to write

My Notes and Drafts

These pages will provide plenty of space for you to take notes on whatever you want. You could also use this space to work on your Writing Workshops first drafts.

My Notes and Drafts

MY NOTES AND DRAFTS

MY NOTES AND DRAFTS

My Notes and Drafts

MY NOTES AND DRAFTS

My Notes and Drafts

My Notes and Drafts

My Notes and Drafts

MY NOTES AND DRAFTS

MY NOTES AND DRAFTS

My Notes and Drafts

MY NOTES AND DRAFTS

My Notes and Drafts

MY NOTES AND DRAFTS

My Notes and Drafts

MY NOTES AND DRAFTS

My Notes and Drafts

My Notes and Drafts

My Notes and Drafts

My Notes and Drafts

MY NOTES AND DRAFTS

My Notes and Drafts

My Notes and Drafts

MY NOTES AND DRAFTS

MY NOTES AND DRAFTS

MY NOTES AND DRAFTS

MY NOTES AND DRAFTS

My Notes and Drafts

My Notes and Drafts

My Notes and Drafts

My Notes and Drafts

MY NOTES AND DRAFTS

My Notes and Drafts

My Notes and Drafts

My Notes and Drafts

My Notes and Drafts

MY NOTES AND DRAFTS

MY NOTES AND DRAFTS

MY NOTES AND DRAFTS

My Notes and Drafts

My Notes and Drafts

My Notes and Drafts

Resources

Word Parts and Academic Vocabulary

Word Parts

Most English words can be broken into smaller units called word parts. The three types of word parts are roots, prefixes, and suffixes. Knowing the meanings of these word parts can help you determine the meanings of many unfamiliar words.

Roots The *root* is the main part of a word. It carries the word's meaning, and it is the part to which prefixes and suffixes are added.

Commonly Used Roots

Roots	Meanings	Examples
–act–	do	action, react
–biblio–, –bibli–	book	bibliography, biblical
–chron–	time	chronology, chronic
–fac–	make	manufacture, factory
–log–, –logue–, –logy–	study, word	logo, biology
–magni–	large	magnitude, magnify
–mal–	bad	malpractice, dismal
–mot–	move	motion, promote
–ped–	foot	pedal, quadruped
–phon–	sound	telephone, phonograph
–sym–, –syn–	with, together	sympathy, syndrome

Prefixes A *prefix* is a word part that is added before a root.

Commonly Used Prefixes

Prefixes	Meanings	Examples
de–	away from, off, down	decode, defend, defuse
dia–	through, across, between	dialogue, diameter
hemi–	half	hemicycle, hemisphere
inter–	between, among	interact, interstate
mis–	badly, not, wrongly	mislead, mistake
non–	not	nonfiction, nonstop
over–	above, excessive	overthrow, overtime
post–	after, following	postdated, postwar
pre–	before	prepare, preview
re–	back, backward, again	replay, return, reverse
sub–, suf–, sum–, sup–, sus–	under, beneath	subplot, suffocate, summon, support, suspend
trans–	across, beyond	translate, transport
un–	not, reverse of	uneven, unspoken

Suffixes A *suffix* is a word part that is added after a root. Adding or changing a suffix will often change both a word's meaning and its part of speech, as in teach/teacher. Teach is a verb. Teacher is a noun.

Commonly Used Suffixes

Suffixes	Meanings	Examples
–ate	to become, to cause	concentrate, vaccinate
–dom	state, condition	freedom, wisdom
–en	made of, to become	sharpen, wooden
–fy	to make, to cause	magnify, terrify
–hood	state, condition	neighborhood, sisterhood
–ible	able, likely	collectible, visible
–ish	tending to be, like	childish, smallish
–ity	state, condition	activity, flexibility
–ize	to make, to cause to be	dramatize, legalize
–ment	result, act of	appointment, payment
–ness	quality, state	darkness, sadness
–ous	characterized by	generous, joyous
–tion	act of, state	flirtation, protection

Academic Vocabulary

INTRODUCTORY COURSE

achieve (uh CHEEV) v.	succeed in getting a good result or in doing something you want.
adapt (uh DAPT) v.	change ideas or behavior to fit a new situation.
adequacy (AD uh kwih see) n.	quality of being enough to meet a need or requirement.
appreciate (uh PREE shee ayt) v.	understand and enjoy the good qualities or value of something.
attitude (AT uh tood) n.	opinions and feelings about someone or something.
authority (uh THAWR uh tee) n.	someone who is respected because of his or her knowledge about a subject.
characteristics (kar ihk tuh RIHS tihks) n.	important, typical parts or features.
circumstance (SUR kuhm stans) n.	event or condition that affects a person.
communicate (kuh MYOO nuh kayt) v.	express thoughts or feelings clearly so that other people understand them.
concept (KAHN sehpt) n.	idea of how something is or could be.
conclude (kuhn KLOOD) v.	decide something after considering all the information.
contribute (kuhn TRIHB yut) v.	give or add something, such as resources or ideas.
contrived (kuhn TRYVD) adj.	unnatural; artificial.
conveyed (kuhn VAYD) v.	made known.
correspond (kawr uh SPOND) v.	be similar to.
crucial (KROO shuhl) adj.	very important.
detect (dih TEHKT) v.	notice or discover, especially something that is not easy to see, hear, and so on.
device (dih VYS) n.	way of achieving a particular purpose.
display (dihs PLAY) v.	show clearly; reveal.
distinct (dihs TIHNGKT) adj.	distinguishable; clearly different or of a different type.

Word Parts and Academic Vocabulary

illustrate (IHL uh strayt) v.	explain or make something clear by giving examples.	**conclude** (kuhn KLOOD) v.	decide by reasoning.
indicate (IHN duh kayt) v.	show; express; suggest.	**delineate** (duh LIHN ee ayt) v.	describe in detail; portray.
influence (IHN flu uhns) n.	ability or power to affect thought, behavior, or development.	**element** (EHL uh muhnt) n.	essential part of something.
insight (IHN syt) n.	clear understanding of the true nature of something.	**explain** (ehk SPLAYN) v.	give reasons for; make understandable.
interact (ihn tuhr AKT) v.	talk to and deal with others.	**extent** (ehk STEHNT) n.	degree to which something extends.
interpret (ihn TUR priht) v.	decide on the meaning of something.	**function** (FUHNGK shuhn) n.	purpose of a specific person or thing.
major (MAY juhr) adj.	very large and important, especially compared with other things of a similar kind.	**identify** (y DEHN tuh fy) v.	recognize and be able to say what someone or something is.
obvious (AHB vee uhs) adj.	easy to notice or understand.	**impact** (IHM pakt) n.	powerful effect.
perceive (puhr SEEV) v.	grasp mentally; understand.	**implicit** (ihm PLIHS iht) adj.	suggested or understood but not stated directly.
perspective (puhr SPEHK tihv) n.	mental view or outlook; way of thinking.	**insight** (IHN syt) n.	power to understand.
qualities (KWAHL uh teez) n.	traits; distinguishing characteristics.	**instance** (IHN stuhns) n.	occurrence or example.
uniform (YOO nuh fawrm) adj.	having the same shape, size, quality, or other characteristics.	**interpret** (ihn TUR priht) v.	explain the meaning of.
visual (VIHZH oo uhl) adj.	related to seeing or to sight.	**narrative** (NAR uh tihv) adj.	that narrates or recounts; being in story form.
FIRST COURSE		**organizational** (AWR guh nuh ZAY shuh nuhl) adj.	pertaining to organization or structure.
advance (ad VANS) v.	move forward.	**perceive** (puhr SEEV) v.	be aware of through the senses; observe.
analyze (AN uh lyz) v.	examine in detail.	**recur** (rih KUR) v.	occur again.
articulate (ahr TIHK yuh layt) v.	express clearly and specifically.	**relevant** (REHL uh vuhnt) adj.	directly relating to the subject.
assess (uh SEHS) v.	examine and judge the value of something; evaluate.	**respond** (rih SPAHND) v.	say or write something as a reply.
attribute (AT ruh byoot) n.	quality or trait of someone or something.	**reveal** (rih VEEL) v.	show something that was previously hidden.
characteristics (kar ihk tuh RIHS tihks) n. pl.	distinguishing qualities or features.	**sequence** (SEE kwuhns) n.	specific order in which things follow one another.
circumstance (SUHR kuhm stans) n.	condition or fact.	**significant** (sihg NIHF uh kuhnt) adj.	important.
comment (KAHM ehnt) v.	make a remark or observation.	**similar** (SIHM uh luhr) adj.	almost the same.
communicate (kuh MYOO nuh kayt) v.	share information or ideas.	**specific** (spih SIHF ihk) adj.	definite and particular.

structure (STRUHK chuhr) n.	the way in which a set of parts is put together to form a whole.	distinctive (dihs TIHNGK tihv) adj.	special; different from others.
technique (tehk NEEK) n.	method of doing a particular task.	elements (EHL uh muhnts) n.	parts of which things are made up.
tradition (truh DIHSH uhn) n.	a set of beliefs or customs that have been handed down for generations.	evaluate (ih VAL yoo ayt) v.	judge.
vision (VIHZH uhn) n.	force or power of imagination.	evident (EHV uh duhnt) adj.	plain; clear; obvious.
SECOND COURSE		expository (ehk SPAHZ uh tawr ee) adj.	containing an explanation.
analyze (AN uh lyz) v.	examine in detail.	factor (FAK tuhr) n.	something that has an influence on something else.
approach (uh PROHCH) n.	method or style of doing something.	insight (IHN syt) n.	understanding of how things work or how people think or act.
articulate (ahr TIHK yuh layt) v.	clearly express in words.	intent (ihn TEHNT) n.	purpose; plan; aim.
aspect (AS pehkt) n.	one part of a situation, plan, or subject.	interact (ihn tuhr AKT) v.	behave toward one another.
associations (uh soh see AY shuhnz) n.	connections in the mind between different things.	interpret (ihn TUR priht) v.	decide the intended meaning of something.
attitude (AT uh tood) n.	way of thinking about or viewing something.	motivation (moh tuh VAY shuhn) n.	reasons behind a person's action or actions.
characteristics (kar ihk tuh RIHS tihks) n.	qualities or features of something.	reaction (ree AK shuhn) n.	action in response to an influence or force.
coherence (koh HIHR uhns) n.	clarity; logical connection.	relevance (REHL uh vuhns) n.	quality of being important or meaningful.
complex (kuhm PLEHKS) adj.	complicated; difficult to understand.	response (rih SPAHNS) n.	reply or reaction.
consistency (kuhn SIHS tuhn see) n.	uniformity; regularity.	significant (sihg NIHF uh kuhnt) adj.	meaningful; important.
contemporary (kuhn TEHM puh rehr ee) adj.	in the style of present time; modern.	specify (SPEHS uh fy) v.	mention or describe in detail; give as a condition.
critical (KRIHT ih kuhl) adj.	vital, very important.	structural (STRUHK chuhr uhl) adj.	associated with the arrangement of parts.
criticism (KRIHT uh sihz uhm) n.	analysis and judgment of a work's strengths and weaknesses	tradition (truh DIHSH uhn) n.	a custom, belief, or way of doing things that is handed down, as in families.
critique (krih TEEK) v.	judge the quality of.	traditional (truh DIHSH uh nuhl) adj.	handed down, usually by word of mouth.
device (dih VYS) n.	method used to produce a specific effect.		

191

Vocabulary Graphic Organizers

You have probably used a lot of graphic organizers over the years. You have used them to take notes on a story you are reading, to compare two countries or trace a time line in your social studies classroom, and to outline causes and effects or a sequence of events for a writing assignment. You can also use graphic organizers to learn vocabulary words. Here are some of those vocabulary graphic organizers. Look them over and use some of them as you take notes on vocabulary words in this notebook.

Definition Map

A Definition Map is a good organizer to use for an academic term. In your social studies class, academic terms might be words or phrases like "monarch" or "political system." In your language arts classes, they might be words or phrases like "symbolism" or "character traits." In a Definition Map, the term you want to remember goes in the center box—in our example, the term is "Historical Fiction." First you write the definition (What is it?). In the boxes on the right, you identify its attributes (characteristics or features). Finally, in the boxes below the term, you provide examples.

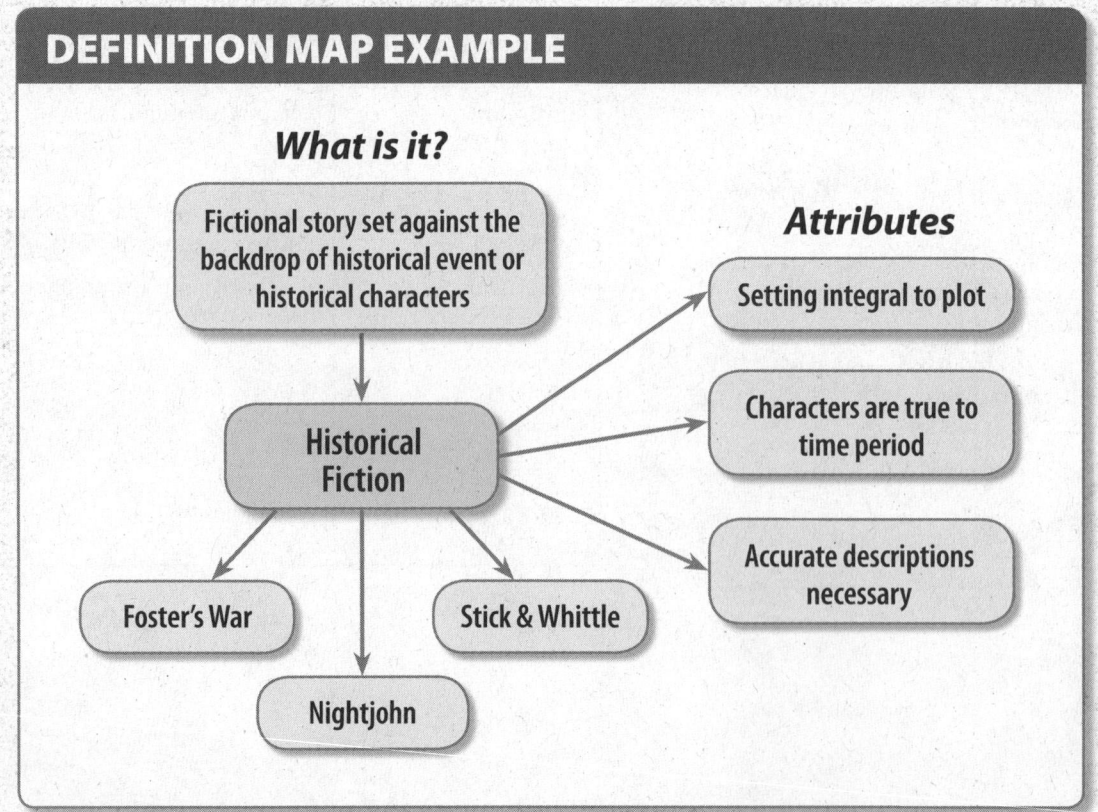

Circle Map

A Circle Map can be used to study and learn any word or term. You start with the word itself, and below the word you create a circle that you divide into four sections. In the top left section, you write the definition. In the top right section, you write a synonym for the word or, if English is your second language, write the word as it is spelled in your first language. In the lower right corner, write an antonym, a word that has the opposite meaning. In the lower left corner, draw some image that will remind you of the meaning of the word. And, finally, write a new sentence using the word.

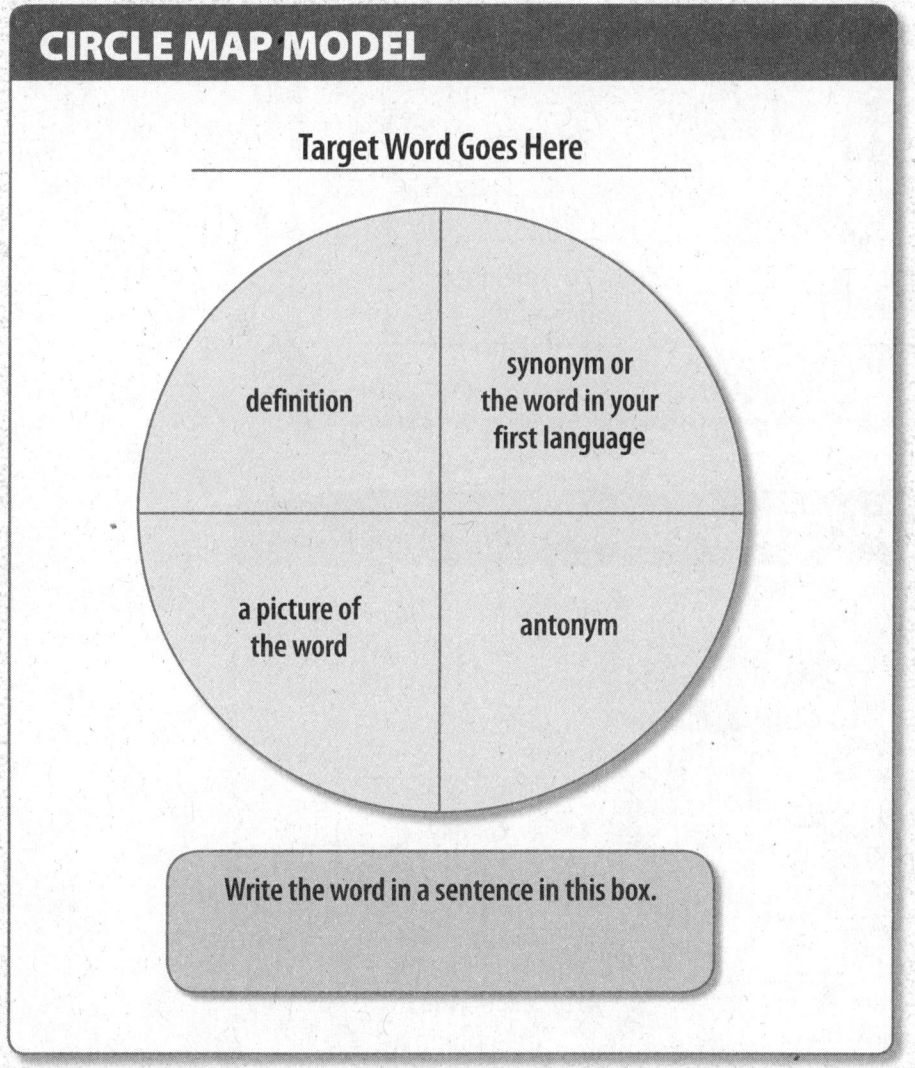

Vocabulary Graphic Organizers

Vocabulary Graphic Organizers

Association Map

An Association Map is a simple graphic organizer that helps you learn the word by making associations between the word and its definition, its synonym, the context in which you might hear it used, and a hint to help you remember it.

ASSOCIATION MAP MODEL

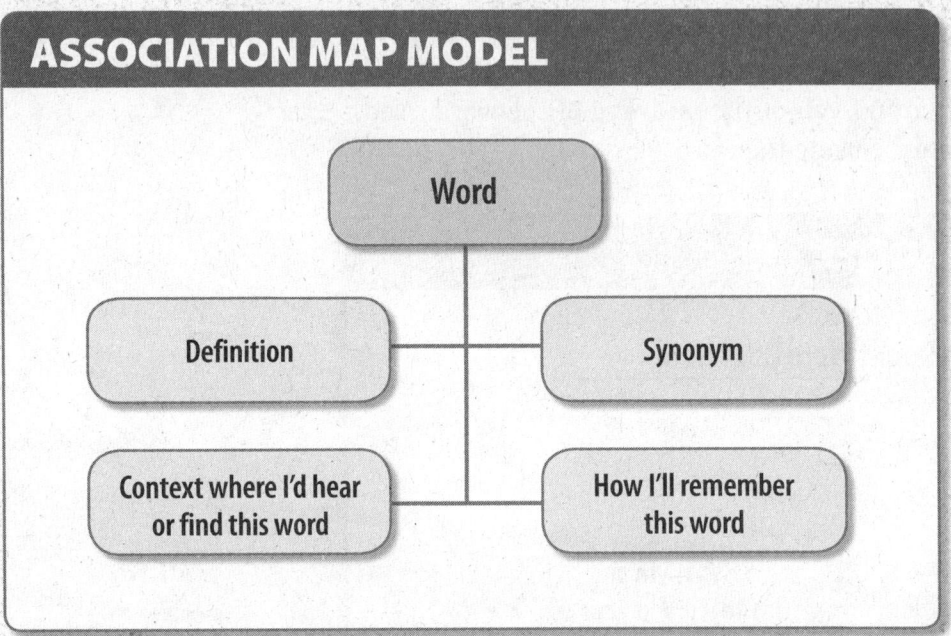

ASSOCIATION MAP EXAMPLE

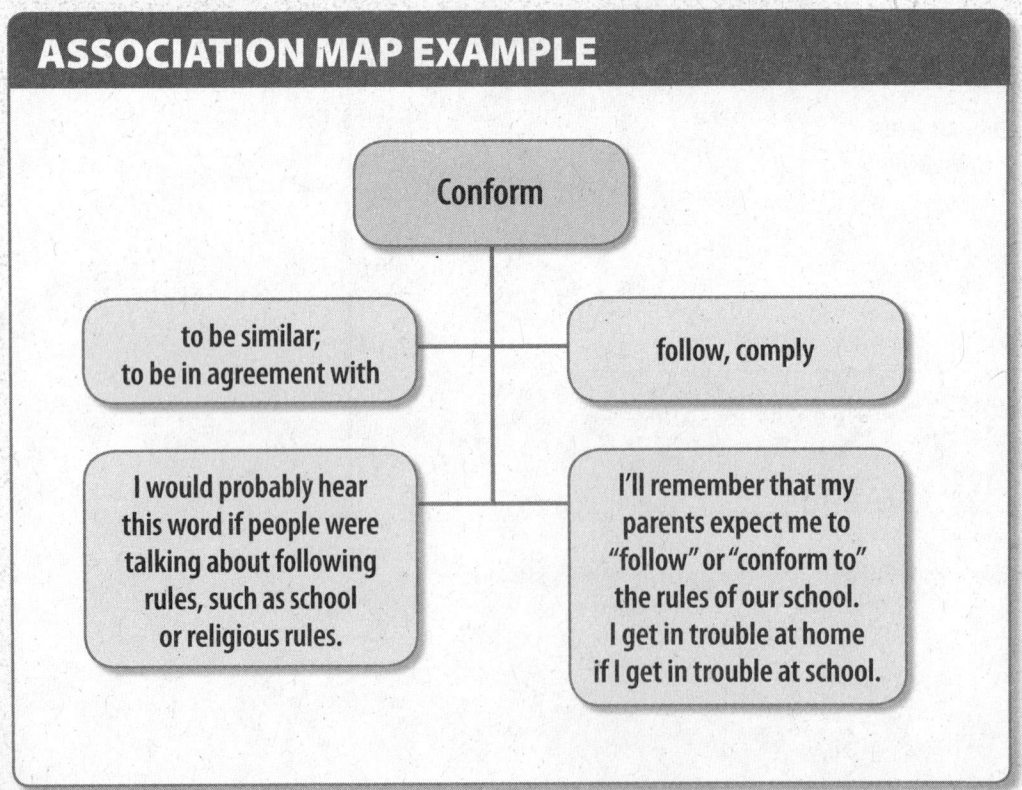

Attribute Map

An Attribute Map follows the format of a graphic organizer that is sometimes called a cluster diagram or a spider map. It will work for any word or term. You simply write the word or term you want to remember in a circle in the middle of the page. Then you draw lines out from that circle to other circles. In each of the other circles you write an attribute of the term. An attribute is a characteristic, or feature, of something else. For example, if the target word or term you want to learn is "setting," you might list the following attributes: time, place, descriptive details, reveals character, suggests theme, and creates an emotional effect or mood.

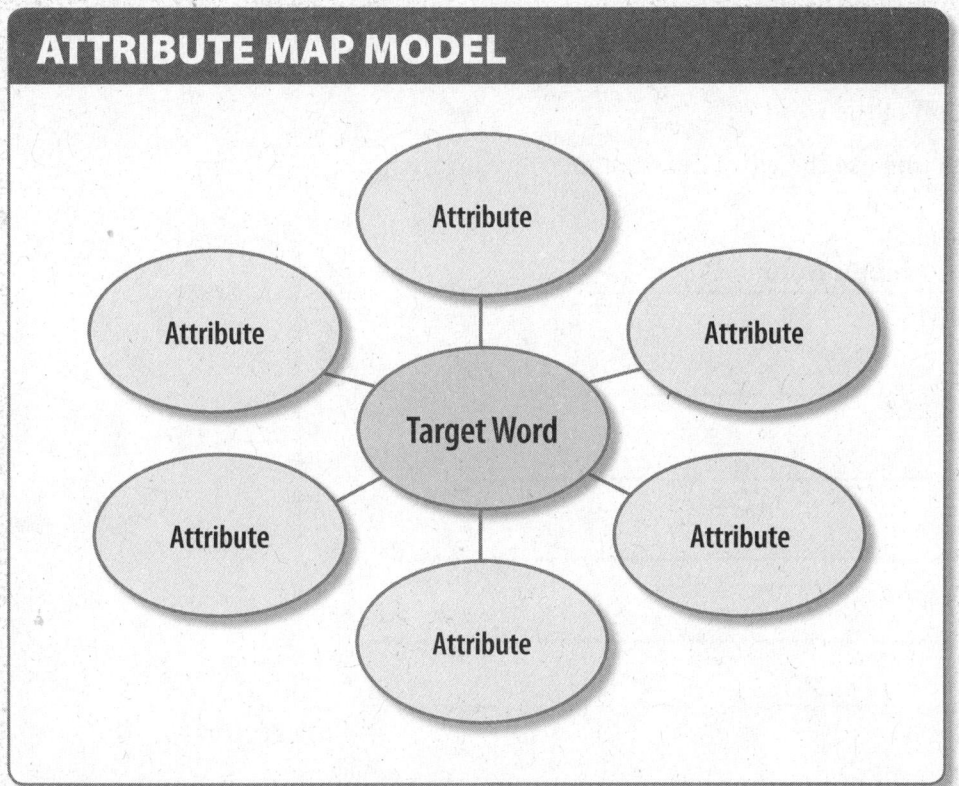

Vocabulary Graphic Organizers

From Context to Context

From Context to Context is a graphic organizer in which you keep expanding the contexts of the word, or the surroundings that can show its meaning. By studying the word in its different contexts, you learn the full meaning of the word and make it your own.

FROM CONTEXT TO CONTEXT MODEL

1. On the first line of the graphic organizer, write a sentence in which you use the word.

2. On the next line (one level down) use your own words to explain your understanding of the word from the context.

3. On the third line (next level down) write the dictionary or thesaurus definition of the word.

4. Finally, on the last line use the word in a sentence of your own.

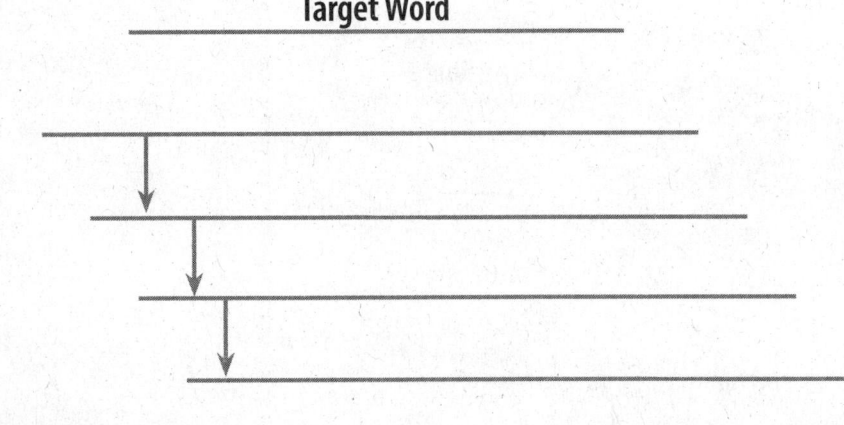

Semantic Map

A Semantic Map is a map of a word or term and its meanings. It can take any shape that makes sense to the person creating the map. In this semantic map, you analyze the word or term you are studying in three ways. First, you identify the class, or group of things your word or term falls into. Then you identify the attributes (characteristics or features) of the word or term. Finally, you identify a number of examples of the concept.

SEMANTIC MAP MODEL

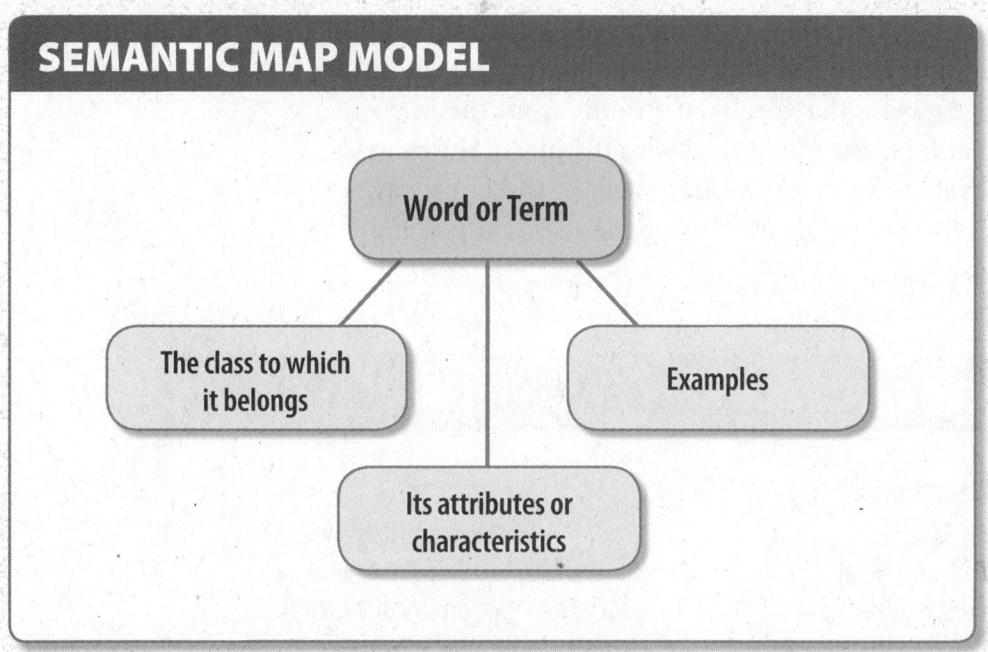

SEMANTIC MAP EXAMPLE

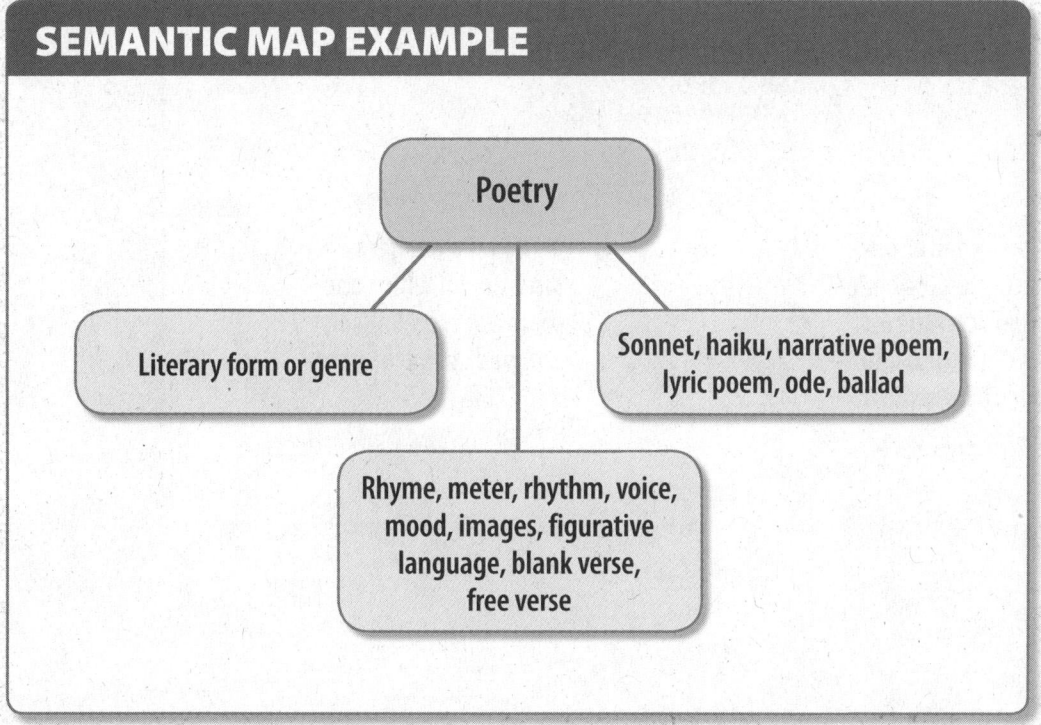

Vocabulary Graphic Organizers

Multi-Word Web or Diagram

A Multi-Word Web or a Multi-Word Diagram is useful when you want to try to learn and remember a number of words at once. For example, when you are reading a chapter in your science or social studies book, you need to try to remember all of the new terms. When you are reading a story or play, you may need to learn a number of new vocabulary words that occur in the selection.

To create a Multi-Word Web or Diagram for the pieces you read in your language arts class, you might start with one of these concepts. For a story, you might start with the name of the story itself, its central character, or its plot, and then create your web or diagram by constructing sentences using the vocabulary words from the selection. For a nonfiction piece, you might start with the title of the essay or the article or with its topic or main idea. Then, in the same way, proceed to construct the web or diagram using the selection vocabulary in related sentences.

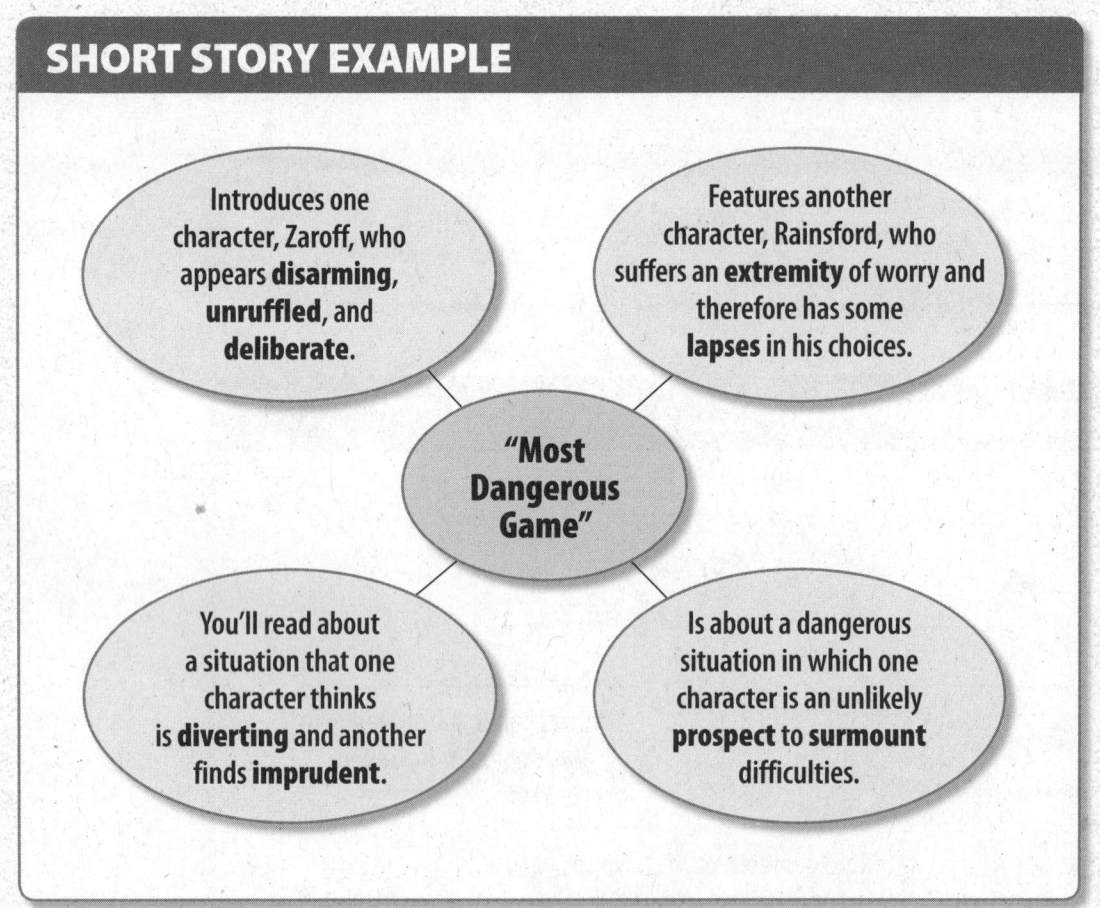

SHORT STORY EXAMPLE

- Introduces one character, Zaroff, who appears **disarming**, **unruffled**, and **deliberate**.
- Features another character, Rainsford, who suffers an **extremity** of worry and therefore has some **lapses** in his choices.
- "Most Dangerous Game"
- You'll read about a situation that one character thinks is **diverting** and another finds **imprudent**.
- Is about a dangerous situation in which one character is an unlikely **prospect** to **surmount** difficulties.

For a nonfiction piece, you might start with the title of the essay or the article or with its topic or main idea. Then, in the same way, proceed to construct the web or diagram using the selection vocabulary in related sentences.

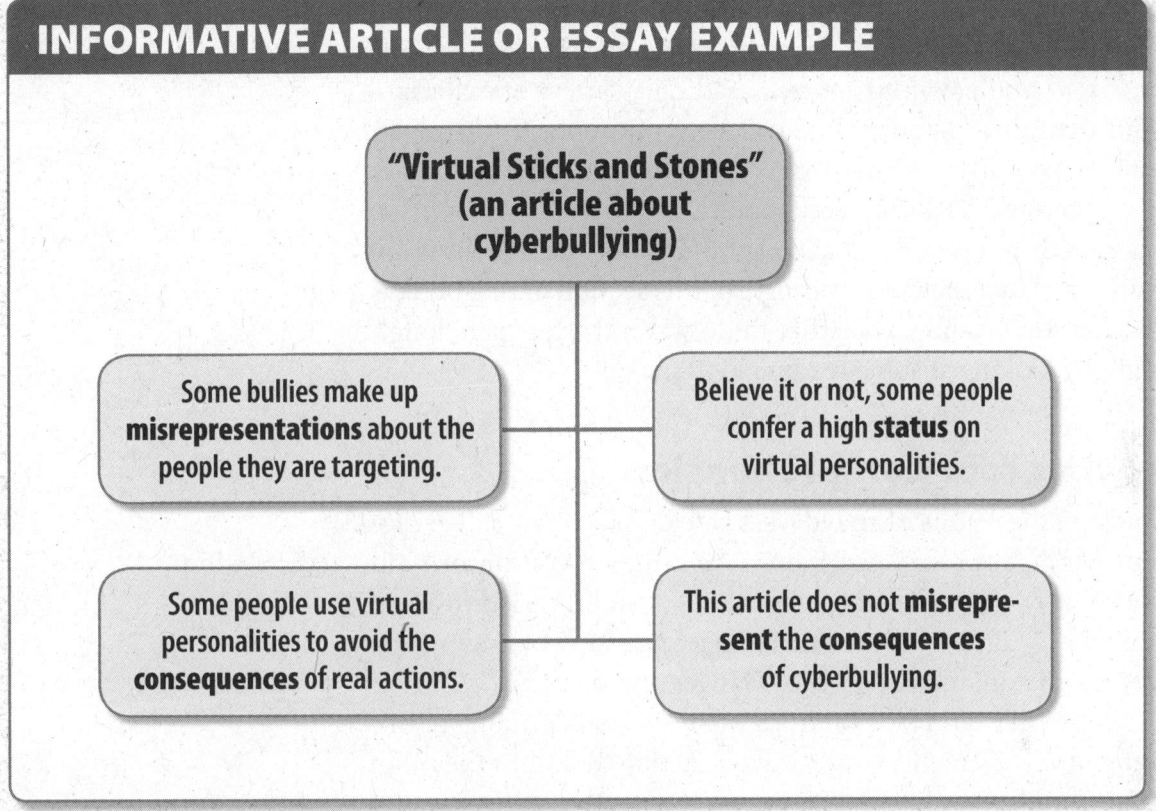

INFORMATIVE ARTICLE OR ESSAY EXAMPLE

Reading Matters
by Kylene Beers

Remember the reading you did back in first, second, and third grades? Big print. Short texts. Easy words. Now, however, the texts you read are often filled with small print, long chapters, and complicated plots or topics. Also, you now find yourself reading a variety of material—from your driver's-ed handbook to college applications, from job applications to income-tax forms, from e-mail to e-zines, from classics to comics, from textbooks to checkbooks.

Doing something every day that you find difficult and tedious is not much fun—and that includes reading. So, this section of this book is designed for you, to show you what to do when the text gets tough. Let's begin by looking at some reading matters.

Improving Your Comprehension

Have you seen the reruns of an old weekly television show called *Lost in Space*? Perhaps you saw the more recent movie version of it? If so, you probably remember the robot that constantly tried to warn the young boy, Will Robinson, when danger was near by waving his robot arms and announcing loudly, "Danger approaching, Will Robinson!" Then Will would look up from whatever he was doing, notice whatever evil was moments away, and take action. But until the robot warned him, Will would ignore all warning signs that danger was at hand.

Wouldn't it be nice if something would warn us as we were about to enter a dangerous area when we were reading—a part of the text that we might not understand? Perhaps our own little robots could pop up in books, saying, "Danger, reader! Misunderstandings approaching!" Then we'd know to slow down, pay attention, and carefully study the text we were reading.

Actually those signs do appear, but not as arm-waving robots in the margins of books. Instead, the signs appear in our minds as we are reading. However, unless we are paying attention, we often read on past them, not noticing the warnings they offer. What we need to do is learn to recognize the danger signs so that like Will Robinson, we will know when to look up and take action.

Danger Sign 1

You cannot remember what you read.

This happens to all readers occasionally. You read something, and your attention wanders for a moment, but your eyes don't quit moving from word to word. In a few minutes you realize you are several pages beyond the last point where you can remember thinking about what you were reading. Then you know you need to back up and start over.

Forgetting what you have read is a danger sign only if it happens to you frequently. If you constantly complete a reading assignment but don't remember anything that you've been reading, then you probably are in the habit of letting your mind focus on something else while your eyes are focusing on the words. That's a habit you need to break.

Tips for Staying Focused

1. Do not read from the beginning of the assignment to the end without pausing. Set up **checkpoints** for yourself, either every few pages or every five minutes. At those checkpoints, stop reading and ask yourself some basic questions—"What's happening now? What do I not understand?"

2. As you read, keep paper and pen close by. **Take notes** as you read, in particular jotting down questions you have about what confuses you, interests you, or perhaps even surprises you.

READING UP CLOSE

Measure Your Attention Quotient Take the following survey to see what your attention quotient is. The lower the score, the less attention you pay to what you are reading.

When I read, I . . .

A. let my mind wander
   1 most of the time
   2 sometimes
   3 almost never

B. forget what I am reading
   1 most of the time
   2 sometimes
   3 almost never

C. get confused and stay confused
   1 most of the time
   2 sometimes
   3 almost never

D. discover I have turned lots of pages and do not have a clue as to what I have read
   1 most of the time
   2 sometimes
   3 almost never

E. rarely finish whatever I am supposed to be reading
   1 most of the time
   2 sometimes
   3 almost never

My Attention Quotient is _____ out of 15.

Reading Matters

Reading Matters

Danger Sign 2

You do not "see" what you are reading.

The ability to visualize—or see in your mind—what you are reading is important for comprehension. To understand how visualizing makes a difference, try this quick test. When you get home, turn on a television to a program you enjoy. Then, turn your back to the television set. How long will you keep "watching" the program that way? Probably not long. Why not? Because it would be boring if you couldn't see what was happening. The same is true of reading: If you can't see in your mind what is happening on the page, then you probably will tune out quickly. You can improve your ability to visualize text by practicing the following strategies:

1. **Read a few sentences; then, pause, and describe what is happening on the page.** Forcing yourself to describe the scene will take some time at first, but it will help in the long run.

2. **On a sheet of paper or a stick-on note, make a graphic representation of what is happening as you are reading.** For instance, if two characters are talking, draw two stick figures with arrows pointing between them to show yourself that they are talking.

3. **Discuss a scene or a part of a chapter with a buddy.** Talk about what you "saw" as you were reading.

4. **Read aloud.** If you are having trouble visualizing the text, it might be because you aren't really "hearing" it. Try reading a portion of your text aloud, using good expression and phrasing. As you hear the words, you may find it easier to see the scenes.

READING UP CLOSE

Visualizing What You Read Read the following excerpt from "Blues, Ain't No Mockin Bird" by Toni Cade Bambara, and discuss what you "see," or can visualize:

"The puddle had frozen over, and me and Cathy went stompin in it. The twins from next door, Tyrone and Terry, were swingin so high out of sight we forgot we were waitin our turn on the tire. Cathy jumped up and came down hard on her heels and started tap-dancin. And the frozen patch splinterin every which way underneath kinda spooky. 'Looks like a plastic spider web,' she said. 'A sort of weird spider, I guess, with many mental problems.' But really it looked like the crystal paperweight Granny kept in the parlor."

> **Danger Sign 3**

You constantly answer "I don't know" to questions at the end of reading selections.

If you consistently do not know the answers to questions about what you have been reading, then you probably would benefit from the following strategies: Think-Aloud, Retelling, Re-reading and Rewording, Somebody Wanted But So, GIST, and Key Words.

Think-Aloud

Comprehension problems do not appear only after you finish reading. Confusion occurs as you read. Therefore, don't wait until you complete your reading assignment to try to understand the text; instead, work on comprehending while reading by becoming an active reader.

Active readers predict, connect, clarify, question, and visualize as they read. If you do not do those things, then you need to pause while you read to

- make predictions
- make connections
- clarify in your own thoughts what you are reading
- question what you do not understand
- visualize the text and observe key details

Use the Think-Aloud strategy to practice your active-reading skills. Read a selection of text aloud to a partner. As you read, pause to make comments and ask questions. Your partner's job is to tally your comments and classify each according to the list above.

> **READING UP CLOSE**
>
> **One Student's Think-Aloud** Here is one student's Think-Aloud for "Cranes" by Hwang Sunwon:
>
> *Sixth paragraph:* In this part, Sŏngsam suddenly sees a childhood friend he used to know. I also saw a friend of mine the other day, and the last time I had seen him was in first grade.
> **(Connection)**
>
> *Eleventh paragraph:* Sŏngsam says, "I'll take the fellow with me." I bet he plans to find out why Tŏkchae joined the Farmers Communist League.
> **(Prediction)**
>
> *Thirteenth paragraph:* Why does Tŏkchae say his father is ill?
> **(Question)**
>
> *Fourth paragraph:* Oh, now I see. Tŏkchae explains that he didn't escape because he didn't want to leave his sick father.
> **(Clarification)**

Reading Matters

Retelling

While the Think-Aloud strategy keeps you focused as you read, the Retelling strategy helps you after reading. Read the tips for retelling below, and then practice retelling small portions of your reading assignments. You might ask a friend to listen to you retell what you have read, or you might record yourself as you retell a selection.

Retelling Prompts for Fiction

1. State what text you are retelling.
2. Give characters' names, and explain who they are.
3. Sequence the events using words like *first*, *second*, *third*, *then*, *later*, *next*, and *last*.
4. Identify the conflict in the story.
5. Explain the resolution of the conflict.
6. Tell what you enjoyed or did not enjoy about the text.

Retelling Prompts for Informational Texts

State what text you are retelling, and identify the structure of the text.

- If the structure is a **sequence** (the water cycle), use words like *first*, *second*, *third*, *then*, *later*, *afterwards*, *following that*, *before*, and *last*.
- If the structure is **comparison and contrast** (the differences between soccer and football), use words or phrases such as *by comparison*, *by contrast*, *on the other hand*, *yet*, *but*, *however*, *nevertheless*, *conversely*, *then again*, or *in opposition*.
- If showing **cause-and-effect relationships**, use words like *reason*, *motive*, *basis*, and *grounds* to discuss **causes**, and use words like *outcome*, *consequence*, *result*, and *product* to discuss **effects**.

READING UP CLOSE

Evaluate Your Retelling Listen to your retelling, and ask yourself:

1. Does my retelling make sense?
2. Does it have enough information?
3. Is the information in the correct order?
4. Could a drawing or a diagram help my retelling?
5. If someone listening to my retelling hadn't read the text, what would that person visualize?
6. To improve my next retelling, should I focus on characters, sequence of events, amount of detail, or general conclusions?

Re-reading and Rewording

The best way to improve your comprehension is simply to re-read. The first time you read something, you get the basic idea of the text. The next time you read it, you revise your understanding. Try thinking of your first reading as a draft—just like the first draft of an essay. As you revise your essay, you are improving your writing. As you revise your reading, you are improving your comprehension.

Sometimes, as you re-read, you find some specific sentences or even passages that you just do not understand. When that is the case, you need to spend some time closely studying those sentences. One effective way to tackle tough text is to reword it:

1. On a sheet of paper, write the sentences that are confusing you.
2. Leave a few blank lines between each line you write.
3. Then, choose the difficult words, and replace them in the space above.
4. While you wouldn't want to reword every line of a text, this is a powerful way to help you understand key sentences.

READING UP CLOSE

One Student's Rewording After ninth-grader Callie read the May 8, 1994 New York Times article "Romeo and Juliet in Bosnia" by Bob Herbert she copied a few sentences she did not understand. After re-reading them, she reworded them, using a thesaurus.

1. "But ~~civilization~~ [society] is ~~an exceedingly fragile enterprise~~ [a very weak thing], and it's ~~especially vulnerable to~~ [really in danger of] the ~~primal madness~~ [primitive craziness] of ~~ethnic~~ [racial] and religious hatreds."

2. "When the madness ~~descended~~ [came down] on Sarajevo, Bosko Brkic faced a ~~cruel dilemma~~ [bad problem]."

Reading Matters

Somebody Wanted But So

Understanding a long piece of text is easier if you can summarize chunks of it. If you are reading a narrative, or a story, then use a strategy called Somebody Wanted But So (SWBS) to help you write a summary of what you are reading. SWBS is a powerful way to think about the characters in a story and note what each did, what conflict each faced, and what the resolution was. As you write an SWBS statement for different characters in the same story, you are forcing yourself to rethink the story from different points of view. By analyzing point of view in this way, you get a better understanding of the impact of the author's choice of narrator.

Here are the steps for writing SWBS statements:

1. Write the words *Somebody*, *Wanted*, *But*, and *So* across four columns.
2. In the "Somebody" column, write a character's name.
3. Then, in the "Wanted" column, write what that character wanted to do.
4. Next, in the "But" column, explain what happened that kept the character from doing what he or she wanted.
5. Finally, in the "So" column, explain the eventual outcome.
6. If you are making an SWBS chart for a long story or novel, you will need to write several statements at different points in the story.

READING UP CLOSE

One Student's SWBS Chart Here is one student's SWBS chart for "The Scarlet Ibis" by James Hurst:

Somebody	Wanted	But	So
Brother	*wanted* Doodle to be like other kids,	*but* Doodle's physical problems kept that from happening,	*so* Brother pushed Doodle too hard and then had to live with guilt when Doodle died.
Doodle	*wanted* to please Brother,	*but* he couldn't do all Brother demanded of him,	*so* he died.

GIST

If summarizing the information in **expository**, or informational, texts is difficult, try a strategy called GIST.

Steps for GIST

1. Divide the text you want to summarize into three or four sections.
2. Read the first section.
3. Draw twenty blank lines on a sheet of paper.
4. Write a summary of the first section of text using exactly twenty words—one word for each blank.
5. Read the next section of text. In your next set of twenty blanks, write a new summary statement that combines your first summary with whatever you want to add from this second section of text. It is important to note that even though you now have two chunks of text to cover, you still have only twenty blanks to fill, not forty.
6. Repeat this one or two more times, depending on how much more text you have. When you are finished, you will have a twenty-word statement that gives you the gist, or overall idea, of what the entire text is about.

READING UP CLOSE

One Student's GIST After reading an article titled, "How Did They Disappear?," one student wrote the following GIST statements:

GIST 1 *(for the first and second paragraphs)*

Some scientists believe the earth's rock layers reveal that dinosaurs became extinct after a comet or asteroid struck the earth.

GIST 2 *(adding the third paragraph)*

Some scientists believe iridium in rock layers indicates a comet or asteroid struck the earth, resulting in the dinosaurs' extinction.

GIST 3 *(completing the page)*

Some scientists believe a comet or asteroid struck Mexico, and the resulting greenhouse effect caused the extinction of the dinosaurs.

Reading Matters

Key Words

Sometimes you do not want to write a summary of what you have been reading. Instead, you just want to jot down some key words to remind yourself about a specific topic. To keep your key words organized, create an alphabetical chart, as in the example below. You can use your computer to make this chart or just grab a pencil and notebook paper. Once your chart is drawn, all you have to do is decide what information to include.

The example below shows how one student used her Key Word chart while reading "Thank You, M'am" by Langston Hughes. She put Roger's name in blue at the top of the page and Mrs. Luella Bates Washington Jones's name in italic. As Meredith read the story and thought of words to describe each character, she put those key character-description words in the correct box in the correct typeface. So, she wrote "*preachy*" in italic (because she thought that word described Mrs. Jones) in the O–P box. She wrote "**ashamed**" in bold (because this word is for Roger) in the A–B box. When completed, a chart like this could be a starting point for writing a paper that compares and contrasts Roger and Mrs. Jones.

READING UP CLOSE

One Student's Key Word Chart Here is a student's partially completed Key Word chart for "Thank You, M'am" by Langston Hughes:

Roger   *Mrs. Luella Bates Washington Jones*

A-B **ashamed**	C-D	E-F	G-H	I-J	K-L
M-N	O-P *preachy*	Q-R	S-T	U-V-W	X-Y-Z

Improving Your Reading Rate

If your reading concerns are more about getting through the words than figuring out the meaning, then this part of Reading Matters is for you.

If you think you are a slow reader, then reading can seem overwhelming. But you can change your **reading rate**—the pace at which you read. All you have to do is practice. The point is not to read so fast that you just rush over words—the I'mgoingtoreadsofastthatallthewordsruntogether approach. Instead, the goal is to find a pace that keeps you moving comfortably through the pages. Why is it important to establish a good reading rate? Check out the math in the box below to see why your silent reading rate counts.

> **Math Problem!**
> If you read 40 words per minute (WPM) and there are 400 words on a page, then how long will it take you to read 1 page? 5 pages? 10 pages? How long will it take if you read 80 WPM? 100 WPM? 200 WPM?

As you figure out the problem, you see that it takes 100 minutes to read 10 pages at the slowest pace and only 20 minutes at the fastest pace. See the chart below for all the times.

	1 page @ 400 words/page	5 pages @ 400 words/page	10 pages @ 400 words/page
40 WPM	10 minutes	50 minutes	100 minutes
80 WPM	5 minutes	25 minutes	50 minutes
100 WPM	4 minutes	20 minutes	40 minutes
200 WPM	2 minutes	10 minutes	20 minutes

Reading Rate and Homework

Now, assume that with literature homework, science homework, and social studies homework, you have 40 pages to read in one night. If you are reading at 40 WPM, you are spending over 6 *hours* just reading the information; but at 100 WPM, you would spend only about 2 hours and 45 minutes. And at 200 WPM, you would finish in 1 hour and 20 minutes.

> **READING UP CLOSE**
>
> **Tips on Varying Your Reading Rate**
> - Increasing your rate does not matter if your comprehension goes down.
> - Do not rush to read fast if that means understanding less.
> - Remember that your rate will vary as your purpose for reading varies. You will read more slowly when you are studying for a test than when you are skimming a text.

Figuring Out Your Reading Rate

To determine your silent-reading rate, you will need three things: a watch or clock with a second hand, a book, and someone who will watch the time for you. Then, follow these steps:

1. Have your friend time you as you begin reading to yourself.
2. Read at your normal rate. Do not speed just because you are being timed.
3. Stop when your friend tells you one minute is up.
4. Count the number of words you read in that minute. Write down that number.
5. Repeat this process several more times, using different passages.
6. Then, add the number of words together, and divide by the number of times you timed yourself. That is your average rate.

READING RATE

One Students Example

1st minute	180 words
2nd minute	215 words
3rd minute	+ 190 words
	585 words ÷ 3 = **195 WPM**

Your Turn

1st minute	_____ words
2nd minute	_____ words
3rd minute	+ _____ words
	_____ words ÷ 3 = _____ WPM

Reading Rate Reminders

You can improve your reading rate by using the following strategies:

1. **Make sure you are not reading just one word at a time with a pause between each word.** Practice phrasing words in your mind as you read. For instance, look at the sample sentences, and pause only where you see the slash marks. One slash (/) means pause a bit. Two slashes (//) mean pause a bit longer.

> **Jack and Jill/ went up the hill/ to fetch a pail of water.// Jack fell down/ and broke his crown/ and Jill came tumbling after.//**

Now, read them again, pausing after each word.

> **Jack/ and/ Jill/ went/ up/ the/ hill/ to/ fetch/ a/ pail/ of/ water.// Jack/ fell/ down/ and/ broke/ his/ crown/ and/ Jill/ came/ tumbling/ after.//**

Do you hear the difference? Word-at-a-time reading is much slower than phrase reading. If you are reading one word at a time, you will want to practice reading by phrases. You can hear good phrasing by listening to a book on tape.

2. **Make sure you are not sounding out each word.** At this point in school, you need to be able to recognize whole words and save the sounding-out strategy for words you have not seen before. In other words, you ought to be able to read material as "material" and not "ma-ter-i-al," but you might need to move more slowly through metacognition so that you read that word as "met-a-cog-ni-tion."

3. **Make sure when you are reading silently that you really are reading silently.** Do not move your lips or read aloud very softly when reading. These habits slow you down. Remember that, if you need to slow down (for instance, when the information you are reading is confusing you), reading aloud to yourself is a smart thing to do. But generally, silent reading means reading silently!

4. **Do not use your finger to point to words as you read.** If you find that you always use your finger to point to words as you read (instead of just occasionally, when you are really concentrating), then you are probably reading one word at a time. Instead, use a bookmark to help yourself stay on the right line, and practice your phrase reading.

5. **As you practice your fluency, remember that the single best way to improve your reading rate is simply to read more!** You will not get better at what you never do. Also, always remember that your rate will vary as your purpose for reading varies. So, time yourself, determine your reading rate, start reading more, and remember these dos and don'ts. Soon you will find that reading too slowly is not a problem anymore.

Test Smarts
by Flo Ota De Lange and Sheri Henderson

Strategies for Taking a Multiple-Choice Test

If you have ever watched a quiz show on TV, you know how multiple-choice tests work. You get a question and (usually) four choices. Your job is to pick the correct one. Easy! (Don't you wish?) Taking multiple-choice tests will get a whole lot easier when you apply these Test Smarts:

- **T**rack your time.
- **E**xpect success.
- **S**tudy the directions.
- **T**ake it all in.

- **S**pot those numbers.
- **M**aster the questions.
- **A**nticipate the answers.
- **R**ely on 50/50.
- **T**ry. Try. Try.
- **S**earch for skips and smudges.

Track Your Time

You race through a test for fear you won't finish, and then you sit watching your hair grow because you finished early, or you realize you have only five minutes left to complete eleven zillion questions. Sound familiar? You can avoid both problems if you take a few minutes before you start to estimate how much time you have for each question. Using all the time you are given can help you avoid making errors. Follow these tips to set **checkpoints**:

- How many questions should be completed when one quarter of the time is gone?
- What should the clock read when you are halfway through the questions?
- If you find yourself behind your checkpoints, you can speed up.
- If you are ahead, you can—and should—slow down.

Expect Success

Top athletes know that attitude affects performance. They learn to deal with their negative thoughts, to get on top of their mental game. So can you! But how? Do you compare yourself with others? Most top athletes will tell you that they compete against only one person: themselves. They know they cannot change another person's performance. Instead, they study their own performance and find ways to improve it. That makes sense for you too. You are older and more experienced than you were the day you took your last big test, right? So review your last scores. Figure out just what you need to do to top that "kid" you used to be. You can!

What if you get anxious? It's OK if you do. A little nervousness will help you focus. Of course, if you're so nervous that you think you might get sick or faint, take time to relax for a few minutes. Calm bodies breathe slowly. You can fool yours into feeling calmer and thinking more clearly by taking a few deep breaths—five slow counts in, five out. Take charge, take five, and then take the test.

Study the Directions

You are ready to go, go, go, but first it's wait, wait, wait. Pencils. Paper. Answer sheets. Lots of directions. Listen! In order to follow directions, you have to know them. Read all test directions as if they contain the key to lifetime happiness and several years' allowance. Then, read them again. Study the answer sheet. How is it laid out? Is it

1
2
3
4

or

1   2   3   4 ?

What about answer choices? Are they arranged

A   B   C   D

or

A   B
C   D ?

Directions count. Be very, very sure you know exactly what to do and how to do it before you make your first mark.

Take It All In

When you finally hear the words "You may begin," briefly **preview the test** to get a mental map of your tasks:

- Know how many questions you have to complete.
- Know where to stop.
- Set your time checkpoints.
- Do the easy sections first; easy questions are worth just as many points as hard ones.

Spot Those Numbers

"I got off by one and spent all my time trying to fix my answer sheet." *Oops.* Make it a habit to

- match the number of each question to the numbered space on the answer sheet every time.
- leave the answer space on your answer sheet blank if you skip a question.
- keep a list of your blank spaces on scratch paper or somewhere else—but not on your answer sheet. The less you have to erase on your answer sheet, the better.

Master the Questions

"I knew that answer, but I thought the question asked something else." Be sure—very sure—that you **know what a question is asking you**. Read the question at least twice before reading the answer choices. Approach it as you would a mystery story or a riddle. Look for clues. Watch especially for words like *not* and *except*—they tell you to look for the choice that is false or different from the other choices or opposite in some way. If you are taking a reading-comprehension test, read the selection, master all the questions, and then re-read the selection. The answers will be likely to pop out the second time around. Remember: A test isn't trying to trick you; it is trying to test your knowledge and your ability to think clearly.

Anticipate the Answers

All right, you now understand the question. Before you read the answer choices, **answer the question yourself. Then, read the choices.** If the answer you gave is among the choices listed, it is probably correct.

Rely on 50/50

"I...have...no...clue." You understand the question. You gave an answer, but your answer is not listed, or perhaps you drew a complete blank. It happens. Time to **make an educated guess**—not a wild guess, but an educated guess. Think about quiz shows again, and you will know the value of the 50/50 play. When two answers are eliminated, the contestant has a 50/50 chance of choosing the correct one. You can use elimination too.

Always read every choice carefully. **Watch out for distracters**—choices that may be true but are too broad, too narrow, or not relevant to the question. Eliminate the least likely choice. Then, eliminate the next, and so on until you find the best one. If two choices seem equally correct, look to see if "All of the above" is an option. If it is, that might be your choice. If no choice seems correct, look for "None of the above."

Try. Try. Try.

Keep at it. **Do not give up.** This sounds obvious, so why say it? You might be surprised by how many students do give up. Think of tests as a kind of marathon. Just as in any marathon, people get bored, tired, hungry, thirsty, hot, discouraged. They may begin to feel sick or develop aches and pains. They decide the test doesn't matter that much. They decide they do not care if it does—there will always be next time; whose idea was this, anyway? They lose focus. Don't do it.

Remember: The last question is worth just as much as the first question, and the questions on a test do not get harder as you go. If the question you just finished was really hard, an easier one is probably coming up soon. Take a deep breath, and keep on slogging. Give it your all, all the way to the finish.

Search for Skips and Smudges

"Hey! I got that one right, and the machine marked it wrong!" If you have ever—ever—had this experience, pay attention! When this happens in class, your teacher can give you the extra point. On a machine-scored test, however, you would lose the point and never know why. So, listen up: All machine-scored answer sheets have a series of lines marching down the side. The machine stops at the first line and scans across it for your answer, stops at the second line, scans, stops at the third line, scans, and so on, all the way to the end. The machine is looking for a dark, heavy mark. If it finds one where it should be, you get the point. What if you left that question blank? A lost point. What if you changed an answer and did not quite get the first mark erased? The machine sees two answers instead of one. A lost point. What if you made a mark to help yourself remember where you skipped an answer? You filled in the answer later but forgot to erase the mark. The machine again sees two marks. Another lost point. What if your marks are not very dark? The machine sees blank spaces. More lost points.

To avoid losing points, take time at the end of the test to make sure you

- did not skip any answers
- gave one answer for each question
- made the marks heavy and dark and within the lines

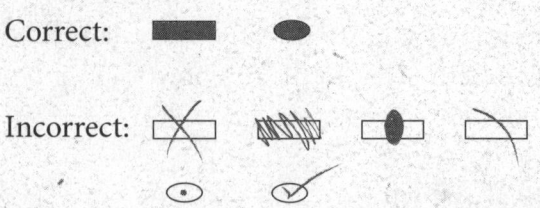

Get rid of smudges. Make sure there are no stray pencil marks on your answer sheet. Cleanly erase those places where you changed your mind. Check for little stray marks from pencil tapping. Check everything. You are the only person who can.

Reading Comprehension

Many tests have a section called **reading comprehension**. The good news is that you do not have to study for this part of the test. Taking a reading-comprehension test is a bit like playing ball. You don't know where the ball will land, so you have to stay alert to all possibilities. However, just as the ball can come at you in only a few ways, there are only a few kinds of questions on reading-comprehension tests. This discussion will help you identify the most common ones. Two kinds of texts are used here. The first one is an informational text. The second is an updated fairy tale.

READING COMPREHENSION

DIRECTIONS: Read the following selection. Then, choose the best answer for each question. Mark each answer on your answer sheet in the square provided.

Night Lights on the High Seas

For centuries, lighthouses have been used to alert sailors that land is near, to point out dangerous rocks and reefs, and to cast a bright light into the night to guide ships on their way. Seafarers have relied on these structures since the days of ancient Egypt. The lighthouse built in 300 B.C. on Pharos, an island near Alexandria, was regarded as one of the Seven Wonders of the World.

Lighthouses help to guide ships at night by giving off an intense beam that flashes every few seconds. Until the eighteenth century, the source of light was an oak-log fire. Coal fire was used for many years after that, until electricity became common in the early twentieth century. Some modern lighthouses also send out radio signals to help ships find their way in foggy weather. Even in their modern form, lighthouses serve their ancient purpose as guiding lights, flashing specks of civilization in the dark, lonely waters of night.

ITEM 1 asks for vocabulary knowledge.

1. In the first paragraph, the word seafarers means —
   A oceans
   B sailors
   C fish
   D ships

Answer: Look at the surrounding sentences, or **context**, to see which definition fits.

A is incorrect. The word *ocean* is another word for "sea," but oceans do not rely on lighthouses.

B is the best answer. In the context of the passage, it makes sense that *sailors* have relied on lighthouses for centuries.

C is incorrect. Fish live and travel in the sea, but nothing in the passage indicates that they depend on lighthouses.

D is incorrect. The safety of ships on the ocean depends on lighthouses. However, it is the *sailors* on the ships who have "relied on these structures" for centuries.

ITEM 2 asks for close reading. Read carefully to see if the answer is stated directly in the text.

2. What was used to produce the light in lighthouses before the eighteenth century?
   F Wood
   G Coal
   H Gas
   J Electricity

Answer: Read the passage carefully to find the answer.

F is the correct answer. The second sentence of the second paragraph indicates that "until the eighteenth century, the source of light was an oak-log fire." The words *oak* and *log* clearly indicate that "wood" is the right choice.

Test Smarts

Test Smarts

ITEM 3 asks for an inference.
3. What is the main idea of this passage?
   A Working in a lighthouse is a dangerous job.
   B Modern lighthouses are very different from those of long ago.
   C The first lighthouse was built in 300 B.C. on the island of Pharos.
   D Lighthouses have helped guide ships for thousands of years.

Answer: Think about which statement covers the passage as a whole.

A is incorrect. The passage does not provide an explanation of working in a lighthouse.

B is incorrect. Lighthouses have not changed that much over the years.

C is incorrect. It is only one detail in the passage.

D is the best answer. It covers most of the details in the passage.

ITEM 4 asks for a prediction.
4. As more and more ships become equipped with navigational computers, what will probably happen?
   F More lighthouses will be built.
   G There will be more shipping accidents.
   H The number of lighthouses will be reduced.
   J Different energy sources will be used in lighthouses.

Answer: Find the information in the passage that supports a probable future outcome.

F is incorrect. Navigational computers will most likely reduce the need for lighthouses.

G is incorrect. The navigational computers will protect the ships from accidents.

H is the best answer. Navigational computers mean that ships will no longer need to rely on lighthouses for guidance.

J is incorrect. The passage does not say anything about new or different energy sources.

ITEM 5 asks you to recognize an opinion.
5. Which is an **opinion** expressed in the passage?
   A The beam from a lighthouse flashes every few seconds.
   B Modern lighthouses send out radio signals.
   C Pharos is an island near Alexandria.
   D The ocean waters are lonely at night.

Answer: A **fact** can be proved true or false. An **opinion**, a personal feeling or belief, cannot be proved true or false. **A, B,** and **C** are facts that can be proved true or false. **D is correct** because it is the only opinion.

ITEM 6 asks you to decide why the author wrote the passage.
6. What is the author's main **purpose** for writing this passage?
   F To entertain readers with an exciting story
   G To inform readers about the history of lighthouses
   H To persuade readers to visit a lighthouse
   J To describe what life in a lighthouse is like

Answer: Look at the information given in the passage, and decide what the writer's purpose was in writing.

F is incorrect. The writer does not tell a story.

G is the best answer. The writer presents information about the function of lighthouses over time.

H is incorrect. The writer's purpose is not to persuade readers to visit a lighthouse.

J is incorrect. The writer never tells what it's like to live in a lighthouse.

READING COMPREHENSION

DIRECTIONS: Read the following selection. Then, choose the best answer for each question. Mark each answer on your answer sheet in the space provided.

A Technologically Correct Fairy Tale: Jack and the Beanstalk

There once was a poor widow who lived in a small cottage with her son, Jack. Jack was a good-hearted fellow who devoted all his time to a mega-computer game. Since Jack did not have a paying job, he and his widowed mother were very poor.

The day arrived when the widow had sold all her possessions via the Internet, except for an elderly cow. Jack was to sell the cow at the market since his mother was too frail to make the trip.

"Get a good price for her," the widow instructed.

"Yes, Mother," Jack answered.

Off he went with the cow in tow.

Out on the highway, Jack was stopped by a man who offered to trade him a handful of oddly shaped, brightly colored beans for the cow. "These are turbo-beans," the man whispered. While Jack didn't know exactly what that meant, he did know that the word *turbo* made the beans sound special, so he agreed to the trade. When he got home, he proudly handed the beans to his mother. She promptly tossed them out the window, declaring she didn't know what he could have been thinking. . . .

ITEM 1 is a vocabulary question. To answer it, consider the surrounding words, or **context,** to identify the best definition.

1. In the first paragraph the underlined word devoted means —
   A donated
   B avoided
   C captured
   D dedicated

A is incorrect. *Donated* means "gave someone something of value." It does not fit in this context.

B is incorrect. It does not fit the context, which shows what Jack did with his time, not what he didn't do.

C is incorrect. It does not fit in the context.

D is the best answer. In this context, *devoted* means "dedicated" or "gave one's time to a particular pursuit."

ITEM 2 is another vocabulary question.

2. In the second paragraph of the fairy tale, frail means —
   F proud
   G weak
   H stubborn
   J forceful

The best answer is G, since it offers the only reason why the widow would not be able to make the trip herself.

ITEM 3 is a factual question. Re-read the fairy tale, and you'll find the answer.

3. How did the widow sell all of her possessions, except for the old cow?
   A She sold them via the Internet.
   B She set up a shop on the highway.
   C She sold them to her neighbors.
   D She sold them to the man with the beans.

A is the best answer. The fairy tale clearly states that she sold her possessions on the Internet.

B is incorrect. Jack met the man with the beans on the main highway. The widow did not go there.

C is incorrect. Neighbors are not mentioned in the selection.

D is incorrect. Jack, not the widow, traded the cow for the beans.

ITEM 4 asks you to analyze a **cause-and-effect** relationship. Do not worry, though. The answer is in the text.

4. Because Jack did not have a paying job, he and his mother were —
    F supported by an uncle
    G very poor
    H reduced to stealing
    J very angry

F is incorrect. An uncle is not mentioned in the story.

G is the best answer. The fairy tale says that they were poor.

H is incorrect. Stealing is not mentioned in the story.

J is incorrect. Anger is not mentioned in the story.

ITEM 5 requires that you make an **inference** based on the text.

5. Jack's mother did not think beans for a cow was a good trade. How do you know this?
    A She explains that a cow is worth more than a handful of beans.
    B Jack was supposed to sell the cow.
    C The man cheated Jack.
    D She tossed the beans out the window.

A is incorrect. Jack's mother does not say this in the story.

B is incorrect. This is true, but it does not explain why his mother didn't think it was a good trade.

C is incorrect. This may be true, but it does not tell us how we know what Jack's mother thought of the trade.

D is the best answer. Her actions show what she thought of the trade.

ITEM 6 asks you to use your **prior knowledge** about fairy tales to predict the outcome of this tale.

6. If this story ended like a typical fairy tale, which of the following predictions would you make?
    F The beans do, indeed, prove worthless.
    G The beans become the key to lifelong happiness for Jack and his mother.
    H The beans end up in a stew.
    J The cow comes home.

F is incorrect. The fairy tale cannot have its "happily ever after" ending if the beans are worthless.

G is the best answer. In fairy tales, magical gifts from strangers often bring great rewards in the end.

H is incorrect. This is too ordinary an ending for a fairy tale.

J is incorrect. This ending is also too ordinary for a fairy tale.

Strategies for Taking Writing Tests

Writing a Story

Some tests may include writing prompts that ask you to write a narrative, or **story**. The following steps will help you write a story. The responses are based on this prompt.

> **PROMPT**
>
> Write a short fictional narrative. The story should include major and minor characters, a thoroughly developed plot, and a definite setting.

STEP 1 Read the prompt carefully. Does the prompt ask you to write a **fictional story** (a made-up story) or an **autobiographical story** (a story of something that really happened to you)?

The word "fictional" tells me that the prompt is asking for a made-up story.

STEP 2 Outline the plot of your narrative. Explain the conflict, the climax, and the resolution.

Conflict—the main character, Sue, wants to win the fencing tournament. Climax—Sue fences against the champion. Resolution—Sue wins but feels bad when she sees her opponent crying.

STEP 3 Identify the major and minor characters. What do they look and act like? How do they sound when they speak?

Major character—Sue is tall and lanky; she is shy; she is very competitive. Minor character—Sue's competitor, Tory, is tall; she is confident and sometimes rude.

STEP 4 Identify the setting of your narrative. Where and when does your story take place?

The story takes place in January during the state fencing championships in a gymnasium.

STEP 5 Draft your narrative, adding dialogue, suspense, and sensory details.

I plan to create suspense by drawing out the moment when Sue must decide what to do when she sees Tory crying. I will use sensory details to describe how she feels. I will also include dialogue of her conversation with Tory.

STEP 6 Revise and proofread your narrative. Make sure that you have organized the events in your story in a logical order. Add transitions that show time, such as *earlier, afterward, at the same time,* and *later*.

Test Smarts

Writing a Summary

Some tests include writing prompts like the one below.

> **PROMPT**
>
> Read the article "The Body's Defenses," and then summarize it. In your summary, include the main idea and significant details of the article.

To write a **summary** of a passage, you rewrite in your own words the passage's main idea and significant details. The summary should both paraphrase and condense the original. A summary of a short passage should be about one-third as long. For a longer selection, a summary should include no more than one sentence for each paragraph.

The following steps will help you write an effective summary in response to a prompt.

STEP 1 Read the passage carefully. Identify the main idea, and restate it in your own words. What is the most important point the writer is making about the topic? How would you say it?

STEP 2 Identify significant details to include in the summary. Which details directly support the main idea? List at least one key idea or detail from each paragraph.

STEP 3 Write the main idea and most significant details in a paragraph, using your own words. Give details in the same order they are presented in the passage.

Writing a Response to Literature

On a writing test, you may be asked to write a **literary response.** Often on such tests, you will be given a literary selection to read and a prompt such as the one below.

> **PROMPT**
>
> What sort of character is Andrew from the short story "Duffy's Jacket"? Analyze his thoughts, actions, and words.

The following steps and the partial student responses will help you respond to a prompt like the one above. The short story "Duffy's Jacket" can be found on pages 5–11.

STEP 1 Read the prompt carefully, noting key words. Key words might include a verb—such as *analyze, identify,* or *explain*—and a literary element—such as plot, character, setting, or theme.

The key words are "analyze" and "character."

STEP 2 Read the selection at least twice. Read first for the overall meaning of the work. Then, read the selection a second time, keeping the key words from the prompt in mind.

STEP 3 Write a main idea statement. Your main idea statement should give the title and author of the work and should directly address the prompt.

Andrew, the narrator of "Duffy's Jacket" by Bruce Coville, is similar to my friend Joss; both are easygoing and funny.

STEP 4 Find specific examples and details from the selection to support your main idea. If you include quotations from the literary work, remember to enclose them in quotation marks.

When Andrew's mom gets mad at Andrew for not reminding Duffy to get his jacket, Andrew thinks to himself, "What do I look like, a walking memo pad?"

STEP 5 Draft, revise, and proofread your response. To create coherence, use transitions between ideas, such as *for example, however,* and *finally.* When you have written your draft, re-read it to make sure you have presented your ideas clearly. Also, check to see that you have fully addressed all the key words in the prompt. Finally, proofread to correct mistakes in spelling, punctuation, and capitalization.

Using the T.H.E.M.E.S. Strategy on a Writing Test

Writing tests often ask you to write a **persuasive essay** in response to a prompt. Most of these prompts give you a topic, but you must identify your position and generate support for your position. Thinking of what to say in a limited amount of time is one of the most difficult parts of such a test.

> **PROMPT**
>
> The city council is considering building a parking garage or a park on an empty lot. Write an essay that takes a position on the issue and defends the position with relevant support.

Use the T.H.E.M.E.S. strategy, explained in the steps below, to generate support for a position quickly. The student responses are based on this prompt.

Each letter in T.H.E.M.E.S. stands for a category you could use to trigger ideas for supporting your position in a persuasive essay.
T=Time   H=Health   E=Education   M=Money   E=Environment   S=Safety

STEP 1 Identify your position on the topic given in the prompt.
   The city council should build a park.

STEP 2 Use T.H.E.M.E.S to list benefits for your position.
   T = A park would take less time to build than a garage. H = People could use the park to exercise and remain healthy. E = People might become more aware, or educated, about the wildlife and plants that occupy the area. M = The city would save money because constructing playscapes and jogging trails is less expensive than clearing the land and building a garage. E = The environment would benefit because the trees and homes of animals are not destroyed. S = Without a garage, fewer cars may drive in the area, reducing the safety hazard of automobile accidents.

STEP 3 Identify the three strongest reasons you developed using T.H.E.M.E.S. Your strongest reasons will be those for which you have the most evidence and those that address readers' concerns about the topic.
   My three strongest reasons for building a park are health benefits, reduced costs, and environmental benefits. These are the issues that I think concern my readers the most.